MW00791766

Bridge's Strangest Hands

Other titles in this series

Boxing's Strangest Fights
Cricket's Strangest Matches
Fishing's Strangest Days
Football's Strangest Matches
Golf's Strangest Rounds
Horse-racing's Strangest Races
The Law's Strangest Cases
Medicine's Strangest Cases
Motor-racing's Strangest Races
Rugby's Strangest Matches
Shooting's Strangest Days
Tennis's Strangest Matches

Bridge's Strangest Hands

ANDREW WARD

ROBSON BOOKS

First published in Great Britain in 2002 by Robson Books, 64 Brewery Road, London N7 9NT

A member of Chrysalis Books plc

British Library Cataloguing in Publication Data
A catalogue record for this title is available from the British Library.

ISBN 1 86105 565 X

Typeset by FiSH Books, London WC1
Printed in Great Britain by Bell & Bain Ltd, Glasgow

Contents

Introduction	ix
A Mississippi Heart Hand (1800s)	1
The Duke of Cumberland Hand (1800s)	2
Elwell's 'Bridge' Tournament (1903)	4
The Elwell Murder (1920)	6
A Matter of Birth and Death (1925)	8
Bridge on the Radio (1926)	10
When Passing Goulash was a Passing Craze (1929)	12
King Amanullah II of Afghanistan (1929)	14
Death by His Own Hand (1929)	16
A Bridge Table Murder (1929)	17
Perfect Hands (1929)	22
Thirteen Hearts but Several Down (1929)	24
Thirteen Hearts and Outbid (1930)	25
The Psychic Bid (1931)	26
The Bridge Battle of the Century (1931–2)	28
The First World Par Olympiad (1932)	31
The Schwab Trophy (1933)	33
The Nullo (1934)	36
Banned by the Police (1934)	38
Stealing Opponents' Slam Bids (1) (1936)	40
Stealing Opponents' Slam Bids (2) (1937)	42
Austria vs. Culbertson (1) (1937)	44
Austria vs. Culbertson (2) (1937)	46
Austria vs. Culbertson (3) (1937)	48

Five-suit Bridge (1937) 51
Midget Bridge (1937) 54
The Beneficial Revoke (1937) 56
The Ladies Beat the Gentlemen (1937) 58
The Complete Misfit (1937) 60
Fourteen Rounds of Bidding (1938) 62
Blindfold Bridge (1939) 65
England Upset by Wales (1939) 68
Cards for Every Occasion (1939) 70
Bridge Rolls and Other Strange Handfuls (1939) 72
Bridge in Battle (1940–5) 74
Prisoner-of-war Camps (1940–5) 76
Everybody Interested (1947) 79
The Raspberry Jam Conundrum (1947) 80
Everybody Off (1947) 82
21 Tricks in Spades (1948) 84
A Straightforward Deal (1948) 86
Too Good to be True (1948) 87
A Heartbreaker (1948) 88
Slam on a Yarborough (1949) 90
Down to the Last Hand (Twice) (1949) 92
Disturbing the Peace (1949) 94
When Defence Claimed 150 Honours (1949) 96
Three No-trumps – Either Way (1950) 98
7,110 Points Resting on the Lead (1951) 100
An International Par Contest (1951) 102
Symmetry (1951) 104
Passing with Over Twenty Points – Lesson 1 (1952) 105
World Champions Knocked Out in First Round (1953) 106
One Diamond, Doubled and Redoubled (1953) 108
Twelve Down for a Penalty of 7,000 (1954) 110
Trio Bridge (1955) 112
The Moonraker Hand (1955) 114
A Ruling in Favour of the Erring Team (1956) 116
The Zero–Zero Fit (1956) 118
The Strange Lead (1958) 120
Twelve of a Suit (1959) 122

Three No-trumps (Redoubled) (1960) 124
The Earthquake of São Paulo (1961) 126
Fact or Fiction? (1961) 128
A Slam Either Way (1962) 132
A Grand Slam Against All Odds (1963) 134
Passing with Over Twenty Points – Lesson 2 (1964) 136
All But Impossible (1964) 138
Another Miracle Hand (1965) 140
The Buenos Aires Affair (1) – Case for the Prosecution (1965) 142
The Buenos Aires Affair (2) – Case for the Defence (1965) 145
The Predictably Unpredictable John Collings (1) (1965) 148
The Predictably Unpredictable John Collings (2) (1960s) 150
Playing Against Genius (1967) 152
When Time Ran Out (1969) 154
The Sharif Bridge Circus (1970) 158
Minus 3,500 (1971) 160
Egdirb (1971) 161
Four Aces or None? (1971) 164
Cars for Cards (1972) 166
A Flat Board? (1973) 168
North or South? (1973) 170
The Bermuda Incident (1975) 172
Hand of the Century? (1975) 175
'Director' (1980) 178
Strange Bidding Systems (1981) 180
On Lead in the Bermuda Bowl Final (1981) 184
An Obvious Sacrifice (1983) 186
A Kidnapping and a Close Finish (1984) 188
Waterloo Station (1985) 191
Same Contract, Very Different Result (1985) 193
Tricks in Batches (1987) 196
A Mammoth Penalty (1987) 198
28 Points and Yet . . . (1988) 200
The Britoil Case (1988) 202
Playing to Lose? (1991) 204
Thirteen Spades (1993) 206

Brazil vs. Norway (1993) 208
The Cat Convention (1993) 210
Everybody's Best Friend (1995) 212
Several Swings (1995) 214
There is Always a First Time (1995) 216
Passing with Over Twenty Points – Lesson 3 (1996) 219
A Tournament Freak (1997) 220
The One–One Fit (1998) 222
The Freakiest Hand (1999) 224
Zia Mahmood Against Seven Computers (1999) 226
International Banned for Cheating (1999) 229
A New Form of Bridge, a New Form of Cheating? (1999) 231
Israel and Palestine (2000) 234
House of Lords vs. House of Commons (2000) 236
A Perfect Hand for Defence (2000) 239
Thrown Out (2000) 240
Strange Conversations (2000) 241
Denmark vs. Spain (2001) 244
Two-person Bridge (2001) 246
The Appeal That Decided the Reisinger Trophy (2001) 250
A Grand Slam from Five Points 253
Joker Bridge (1) (2001) 254
Joker Bridge (2) (2001) 256
Bridge for Six (2002) 258
Massacre at the Table (2002) 260
How to Deal a Perfect Hand 261
Selected Bibliography 263

Introduction

When I told bridge players that I was writing a book on strange hands, everyone had a story to tell.

'I bid Two Spades and our parrot said, "Double". My partner redoubled, and it took a while to sort it all out.'

'We had a lightning competition – three minutes for each hand rather than seven.'

'Then we had a power cut but we found some candles for the last rubber.'

'You should have been at our club last Tuesday. Every hand was strange.'

One of the pleasures of bridge is that virtually every deal has some quality of strangeness – the next hand at your table could be a candidate for a book like this. The problem is that very few of these unique hands are documented and it is difficult to research the *all-time* strangest. What follows, therefore, is not a definitive collection but a range of oddities. It shows how bridge has played its part in embezzlement, murder, suicide, kidnapping, imprisonment and battle, and it demonstrates how the game has provided much enjoyment, laughter and sheer entertainment.

Wherever possible I have tried to choose hands that are not well known, although it is hard to ignore the likes of the Bennett murder and the Duke of Cumberland heartbreaker. Some hands have been included to represent recognisable categories (the complete misfit, the partnership misunderstanding, strange bidding systems), while others are highly individual. Some hands are strange because of their background circumstances (a woman in labour, the serving of raspberry tarts at a crucial stage) and others feature adaptations of the game (five-suit bridge, midget bridge, *egdirb*). You may not have picked up thirteen spades in your bridge career, or bid Six Nullos, but here you can live through the experience of those who have.

I have tried to limit the number of hands with freak distributions, but inevitably a few have crept in. I have also tried to steer clear of very technical hands. Do not anticipate demonstrations of clash squeezes or complex double-dummy problems, but some hands do set interesting questions. Nor is this a book about personalities, although I have occasionally mentioned names.

I have tried to verify each hand, but inevitably there were times when I was dependent on one source. I have rotated some hands so that South is usually declarer. My information comes from a wide selection of bridge writers, right from the stalwarts of the 1920s and 1930s, like Yarborough of the *Sunday Times* and Major Tierce of the *Glasgow Herald*, through the columnists of key publications – *Bridge*, *Bridge Magazine*, *Bridge Plus*, *Bridge World*, *Contract Bridge Journal*, *European Bridge Review* – to modern-day experts.

I am particularly grateful to David Davies and Ann Lee, who shared the research with me, and I also acknowledge help from Marcus Benorthan, Phil Blanchard, Judy Chance, Alan Jenkins, Barbara Jenkins, Dr Joe Metz, Teresa Montoya, Andrew Potter, Alan Thompson, Helen Thompson and the staff of the Bodleian Library, Oxford (especially those in Modern Papers). I would also like to thank all those people who have played bridge with me over the years, in particular Bob, Caro, Derek, Jan, Jane, Margaret, Michael, Mike, Neil, Norman, Penny, Rosemary, Rupert, Sue and Sue.

A MISSISSIPPI HEART HAND

USA, 1800s

Mississippi Heart Hands were set up by cardsharps to lure victims into a betting trap. Although best documented for whist games, with professional gamblers on the Mississippi River steamboats preying on unsuspecting travellers, they are also known in bridge. The most common is the hand shown here. South has a powerhouse hand and is willing to bet his last dollar.

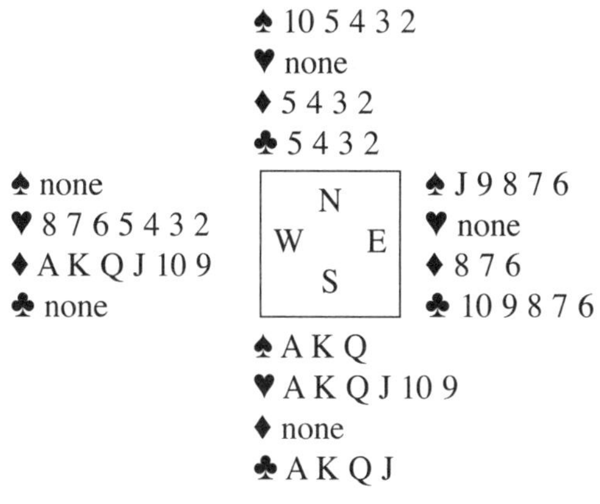

He believes he is invincible but there is no game to be made. A diamond lead restricts South to six tricks in a heart contract.

THE DUKE OF CUMBERLAND HAND

BATH, 1800s

'The following remarkable hand of cards was dealt to the Duke of Cumberland as he was playing at whist at the rooms at Bath, by which he lost a wager of £20,000, not winning one trick,' says Richard Proctor in his book *How to Play Whist* (1885). The deal has passed from whist history into bridge folklore, and a similar coup appeared in Ian Fleming's fiction (see page 114). The Duke of Cumberland in question was probably the son of King George III.

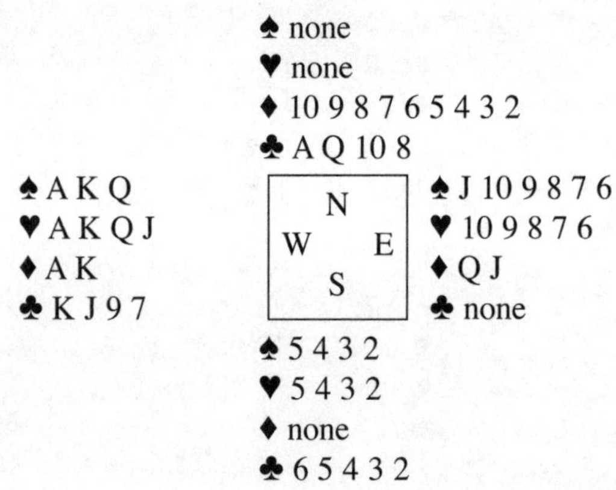

Clubs were trumps and the Duke of Cumberland (West) led a small trump. 'Ninety-nine players out of a hundred would lead trumps,' says Proctor. 'And in my opinion the hundredth would lead wrongly.'

The lead of ♣7 was covered by ♣8, which won the trick. A diamond was ruffed, a second club finessed and another diamond ruffed to return to the hand. A third club was finessed and then North's ♣A could drop the Duke's last club. The last seven diamonds were good, making thirteen tricks.

The hand is worthy of a place in the archives of gambling coups. The Duke of Cumberland probably knew that the hand was staged but still thought he could win a trick.

ELWELL'S 'BRIDGE' TOURNAMENT

NEW YORK CITY, 1903

Whist-bridge expert Joseph Elwell ran a twelve-hand tournament for the *New York Evening Telegram*. An estimated 15,000 people entered the competition and Elwell judged their entries for the best play of the hands.

Here is one of the layouts. South is declarer in No-trumps and West leads ♠7. What is the best way to proceed with the play? Twenty-two readers submitted what Elwell felt was the correct solution. Bear in mind that bridge-whist points were scored for all tricks won, but South's first concern should be to make a game in No-trumps (ten tricks).

Love All. Dealer South.

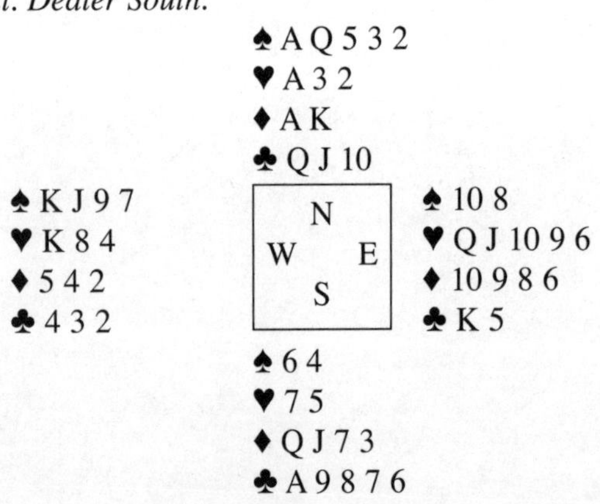

Given West's lead of ♠7, Joseph Elwell felt it unwise to take the spade finesse, in case East could win ♠K and threaten game by making the devastating switch to a heart. Instead, declarer should win ♠A and unblock by playing ♦A and ♦K. This should be followed by ♣10. If East plays ♣K, cover with the ace and throw away two clubs on the two diamond winners (queen and jack). Then run the clubs.

If East does not cover ♣Q with ♣K, let ♣Q run and play another club to the ace, throwing away one club on a diamond winner. After winning the first ten tricks (♠A, five clubs, four diamonds) and thus guaranteeing game, South's lead of a low spade, at trick eleven, also guarantees tricks for ♥A and ♠Q, making twelve in all.

Joseph Elwell later organised more tournaments, but his name made the newspapers for other reasons too…

THE ELWELL MURDER

NEW YORK CITY, JUNE 1920

One of the strangest hands in bridge history was the one that murdered Joseph Elwell in his New York City apartment.

Elwell was a renowned bridge expert and teacher in the days of whist bridge and auction bridge. He wrote a number of books and regularly partnered Harold Vanderbilt, who went on to draft the first outline for the game of contract bridge in 1925.

Elwell's death, in his mid-forties, was 'one of the most celebrated murders of the century', according to John Clay in *Tales from the Bridge Table* (1998). The crime led to a huge number of books and articles, but the police were unable to find enough evidence to prosecute anyone.

'For the first time since Joseph Elwell's death, the game-rooms were deserted,' wrote C C Nicolet in his fictional *Death of a Bridge Expert* (1933). 'The lounges were crowded with excited groups discussing far-fetched theories, and worrying over impending scandal.'

The case was a fascinating story of intrigue that took the police into every area of Elwell's life in search of the murderer. They investigated spurned lovers, family members cut out of the victim's will, husbands of women he had seduced, Wall Street dealers, underworld bootleggers, baccarat players, the horseracing community and, of course, the world of bridge.

According to his estranged wife, Elwell made $1,000 to $10,000 (£200 to £2,000) a night playing bridge at clubs like the Whist Club of New York. His books brought in royalties of $5,000 to $8,000 annually, and he earned about $18,000 a year teaching young society people how to play auction bridge.

On the evening of 10 June, Elwell was the guest of Mr and Mrs Walter Lewisham. They dined at the Ritz-Carlton Hotel, attended the theatre and ended up at Ziegfeld's Midnight Frolic. The fourth member of their party, Viola Kraus, was celebrating her divorce. Curiously, her former husband, Victor von Schlegell, and his new fiancée were also at the Ritz-Carlton and Ziegfeld's that evening.

Elwell arrived home alone at about 2.45 a.m. When his housekeeper arrived at 9 the next morning she found him unconscious and dying in a chair in his pyjamas. He had been shot through the forehead. There was no trace of the gun.

A letter that had been delivered shortly after 7.30 that morning was lying opened at his left side. It was from a racehorse trainer who was responsible for some of Elwell's twenty horses. The murder had therefore occurred between 7.30 a.m., when the post had been delivered, and 9 a.m., when the housekeeper arrived.

Robbery was ruled out as a motive – valuables were untouched – and there was no sign of an intruder. It seemed likely that a close acquaintance was responsible. Several women with keys to the house had been coming and going at will. The housekeeper later admitted shielding one of them, mysteriously referred to as 'Miss Wilson', by hiding a pink silk nightrobe, boudoir cap and slippers that had been left at Elwell's apartment. Elwell had separated from his wife four years previously. He had been shot at by a society woman before, in 1904.

The Elwell case is not the only unsolved murder of a top American bridge player. In 1985 Barry Crane was killed in his California home. Crane, a Hollywood producer responsible for television shows such as *Mission: Impossible*, was perhaps the greatest pairs player and master points-winner of all time.

A MATTER OF BIRTH AND DEATH

BOSTON, MASSACHUSETTS, FEBRUARY 1925

Jack Lemmon was one of the most popular comic and dramatic actors of his day, starring in films like *Some Like It Hot* (1959), *The Odd Couple* (1967), *Save the Tiger* (1973), *Missing* (1982) and *Glengarry Glen Ross* (1992). He features in this book because he owed the circumstances of his birth to a game of bridge.

John Uhler Lemmon III was born in a lift after his mother's trip to hospital had been delayed by a bridge game at the Ritz-Carlton Hotel. Mildred Lemmon was a bridge fanatic who continued her game until labour pains forced her to stop. She was rushed to hospital, where the lift stuck between floors for ten minutes. During that time the young Lemmon arrived. The baby, two months premature, was suffering from jaundice and a nurse remarked that he was 'a yellow Lemmon'.

There are countless stories of bridge interfering with life. In 1947 the pianist Mark Hambourg suffered a serious leg injury when he was accidentally kicked at the bridge table – he took the stage for his next concert in a wheelchair – and King Edward VII reputedly played bridge in the royal train, putting the cards away when he passed through a station so that he could wave from the window of his carriage as if he had been reading the *Methodist Weekly*. Then there is the story of four bridge addicts who travelled by train to a weekend bridge congress. Unfortunately they missed their stop because they were concentrating on the bridge game they were playing.

'According to officials, you cannot drop out of an event unless you die,' said Patricia Fox Sheinwold, commenting on the tournament scene. 'And this seems to be the attitude of the addicts as well. One lady tripped as she walked into the bridge room, played the afternoon session and then had her broken ankle attended to. During a tournament on Long Island a fire broke out and one player refused to evacuate the hotel until he had finished a slam hand that would guarantee his victory.'

Bridge tables have also formed the setting for death – not only premature deaths, like the Bennett murder (see page 17), but those from natural causes. The victims include top-class players, such as American Hal Sims, who died at the table in February 1949, and an England international who died during a congress in Spain. One club stalwart in the north of England helped his partner into a contract of Six Hearts, put his dummy down and then said he was going for a glass of water. When he came back, his partner explained that the contract had been made. 'I thought it would,' he said, and then sat down in a nearby easy chair and died.

In 1930 a Hungarian countess, Aladar Jankovich, died from an apoplectic fit after what was called 'a lively postmortem' on the playing of a particular hand.

In *The Bridge Fiend* (1909), Arthur Loring-Bruce tells an old story about a family of four – father, mother, daughter and son – who frequently played rubber bridge together. During one particularly long session the father collapsed and died from a heart attack. The family immediately began discussing funeral arrangements. The daughter felt that her father would have wished to be cremated, whereas the son was thinking in terms of burial in the family plot.

'I think it should be up to you, Mother,' the daughter said finally.

The mother sobbed before she spoke.

'Up to me?' She checked. 'One Spade.'

BRIDGE ON THE RADIO

USA, OCTOBER 1926

> Each player should take the name of one of the experts and occupy his place at the table.

So started one particular episode of a bridge series that was broadcast on various radio stations around the United States. The experts on this occasion were Sidney Lenz, E V Shepard, Wilbur Whitehead and Milton Work.

> You should have a pack of cards on the table which is divided into suits, so that the cards of each suit may be easily and quickly selected and handed to the proper player. Spread the four suits out on the table, face up, with each suit arranged in sequence, two, three, four, five, six, seven, eight, nine, ten, jack, queen, king and ace.

Dealer North.

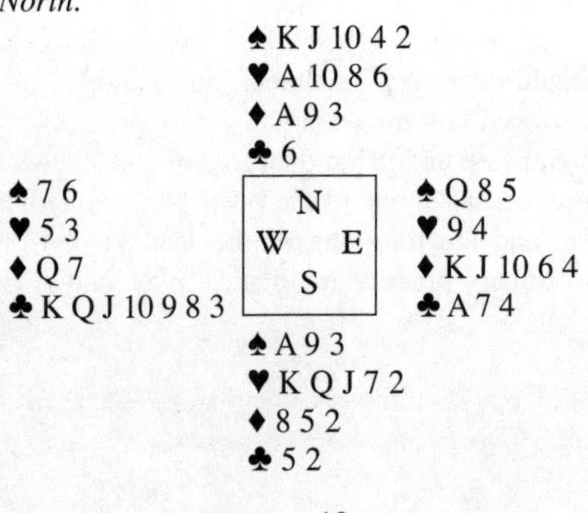

West	**North**	**East**	**South**
Shepard	*Lenz*	*Work*	*Whitehead*
	1 ♠	2 ♦	2 ♠
3 ♣	3 ♠	4 ♣	4 ♥
All Pass			

Each bid was accompanied by a lengthy description of what was happening in the expert's mind. Then the listeners were given the next instruction.

> Each player should now play each card as it is called, placing it immediately in front of him on the table, so that his hand is kept intact. Please do not gather your cards in tricks, but place them in front of you face up.

West led ♣K. North (Lenz) put down dummy and South (Whitehead) studied his options before losing this first trick. He knew he had one club loser, two diamond losers and possibly a spade.

Whitehead won the diamond return with dummy's ace and then set about two rounds of hearts, ending in his hand. He ruffed a club and led ♦3 to East's ♦K.

East was forced to lead a spade, a club or a diamond. None of them would help the defence. Declarer could either trump in dummy and discard his spade loser, or promote dummy's ♠J.

Similarly, if West takes the diamond trick, his next lead ensures the contract makes.

The radio programme then summarised the unusual features of the hand, ending with the week's major lesson.

> This procedure of first taking out the cards of at least two suits in order to force a lead of one of the other two, the avoidance of the finesse, and the throwing of the lead to one of the opponents is ordinary practice in advance play, and is called stripping the hand.

It wasn't a particularly strange hand in itself. What was strange was its dissemination to so many Americans.

WHEN PASSING GOULASH WAS A PASSING CRAZE

USA, 1929

This may be the only time in bridge history when a player was dealt thirteen spades but the opposition bid and made Seven Hearts. It occurred during a special kind of goulash game and we can rely on goulash deals to provide the unusual.

As R F Foster wrote in *Foster's Contract Bridge* (1927):

> This is a variation for four players which differs from contract in one particular. This is that if the highest bid made is not enough to reach game the hand is not played. This condition precludes the possibility of any partial scores, because if game is not both bid and made, nothing is scored but penalties.
>
> If the hand is not played, each person sorts his thirteen cards into suits, and the four hands are then placed one on top of the other and presented to be cut without any shuffling, and are dealt out five–five–three at a time, instead of one by one.

In practice, cards are often dealt out four–three–three–three and this variant sometimes provides complete suits.

Other goulash variations involve passing cards to one's partner at the conclusion of the deal – four cards at the same time, or six cards in three batches (three at first, two next and then one more). But the popularity of 'passing goulash' must have slumped after news of this particular hand. It was dealt during a game where the players had agreed to pass four cards to their partners. At the end of the hand, the lady sitting South was carried out in a dead faint.

East's hand (before and after passing four cards) was given in the *Bridge World* (October 1929), but I have guessed the other holdings. The deal was something like this:

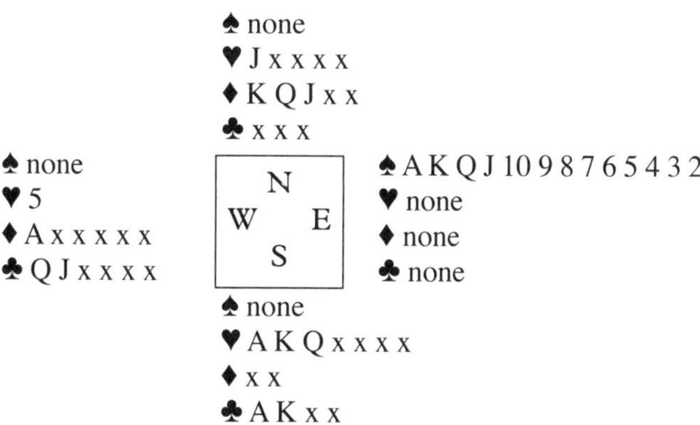

Imagine East's pain. Having been dealt thirteen spades, she now had to pass four to her partner. In return she received a motley selection. Meanwhile, let us imagine that North tried to clear out of clubs and South passed over two low cards in each minor suit. This is how the hands now looked:

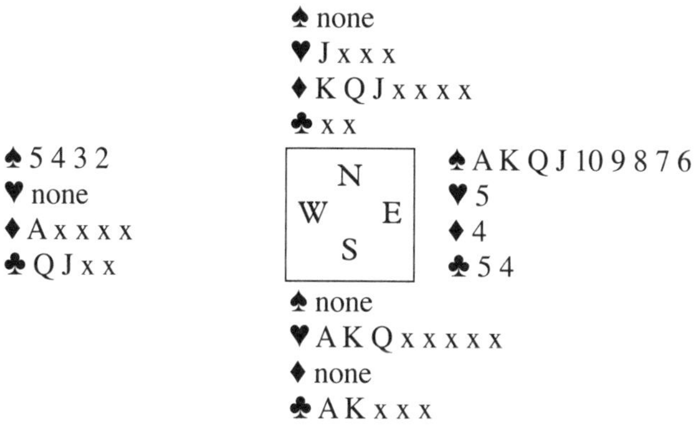

North–South bid to Seven Hearts and the contract sailed home. No wonder East fainted.

KING AMANULLAH II OF AFGHANISTAN

AFGHANISTAN, 1929

When King Amanullah II fled to Europe in 1929, his story became part of bridge folklore.

According to the *Bridge World* (October 1929):

> It has fallen to the lot of Amanullah II, former King of Afghanistan, to lose his throne partly on account of unbridled passion for auction bridge. Perhaps some wily Englishman taught him the fatal game. The fact remains that the King is a passionate bridge fan. I do not know how true it is, but one of his former bridge partners tells me that a friend once saved his head simply because His Majesty despises a three-handed bridge game. His Mohammedan subjects frowned severely upon this infidel pastime: when they learned that four figures of women were actually painted on the cards their rage reached the boiling point where a revolution is ripe. With orthodox Mohammedans it is a gross sacrilege to paint unveiled women in pictures.

Amanullah II took control of Afghanistan in 1919 after his father, Habibullah, died mysteriously during a hunting trip. The country was an emirate at the time – it did not become a kingdom until 1923 – and Britain still controlled foreign policy. One of Amanullah's first actions was to try to liberate Afghanistan. The Third Anglo-Afghan War (1919) ended in military stalemate, but the British conceded decisions of foreign policy. Afghanistan was united and Muslim pride enhanced.

Amanullah was fiercely opposed to British imperialism, but he sought to modernise his country through reforms inspired by those of the West and the pace of change quickened after a trip to Europe and the Middle East in 1928. He may have been taught bridge when he visited England on that trip, or by a British envoy in Kabul, or the game could have made its way across the border from Turkey.

Leon Poullada, in his book *Reform and Rebellion in Afghanistan, 1919–29* (1973), describes Amanullah as a complex and mysterious character. He played tennis, read voraciously and enjoyed hunting and shooting, but there is no mention of bridge. Indeed, the picture of the King in the early 1920s is that of a hard-working leader who put in thirteen hours' work each day and had spare time only for meals, prayers and a horse-ride or drive in the car.

Amanullah's fall was probably less to do with bridge and more to do with underestimating the power of local chieftains. 'The normal regime for Afghanistan is anarchy,' wrote Maurice Fouchet, the first French minister to the court of Kabul, in 1924, 'and the genius of Amanullah must somehow impose the rule of his will on the tribes which are the effective masters of most of the country.'

Amanullah failed to convince the tribal leaders of the need to emancipate Afghan women by outlawing purdah, polygamy and child marriages, and he abdicated in January 1929. He left Afghanistan a few months later and remained in exile in Italy and Switzerland until his death in 1960. Maybe someone remembers partnering him at the bridge table during that time.

DEATH BY HIS OWN HAND

CHAPEL HILL, NORTH CAROLINA, AUGUST 1929

Harry Meacham, a 21-year-old student at the University of North Carolina, was having bad luck with his cards. He had been playing bridge all afternoon and one poor hand followed another.

'I'm going to shoot the next person who deals me a sorry hand,' he said, placing a pistol on the table.

It was Meacham's deal next. He went through the usual procedure and started picking up his cards. It looked like another bad hand. In fact it was a yarborough.

Meacham laid down his hand, picked up his pistol and shot himself in the right temple. He died a few hours later.

That same year, in Detroit, a woman shot her partner (a woman) for pulling out the wrong card twice in a row.

Table rage.

A BRIDGE TABLE MURDER

KANSAS CITY, MISSOURI, SEPTEMBER 1929

Myrtle Adkins first decided that she would marry John Bennett when she saw his photograph at a friend's house, although she did not meet him until much later. She recognised Bennett, who was dressed in officers' uniform, on a train during the First World War, approached him and explained about the photograph. They were married in November 1918. Myrtle Bennett fired the gun that killed John Bennett after an argument at the bridge table.

At the time of his death, Bennett was a prosperous 36-year-old perfume salesman. He and his wife lived in a large Park Manor apartment on Ward Parkway in a salubrious area of Kansas City with Myrtle's mother, Alice Adkins. Their bridge opponents on the fateful day, Charles and Myrna Hoffman, lived in the same apartment building.

On Sunday 29 September, the Bennetts and the Hoffmans made up a foursome for golf during the day and then arranged a bridge game for small stakes in the evening. During the first hour or two of bridge, the Bennetts took a healthy lead. As the game wore on, however, the Hoffmans pegged back the points. When it came to the crucial hand, there was little to choose between the two pairs, except that the Bennetts were doing far more arguing.

The three survivors later agreed on the bidding up to Four Spades, but the sources are divided about whether Charles Hoffman doubled. The survivors were uncertain about the composition of the actual hand when a reconstruction was attempted later, but that did not stop this hand from becoming legendary.

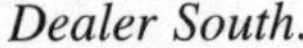

Dealer South.

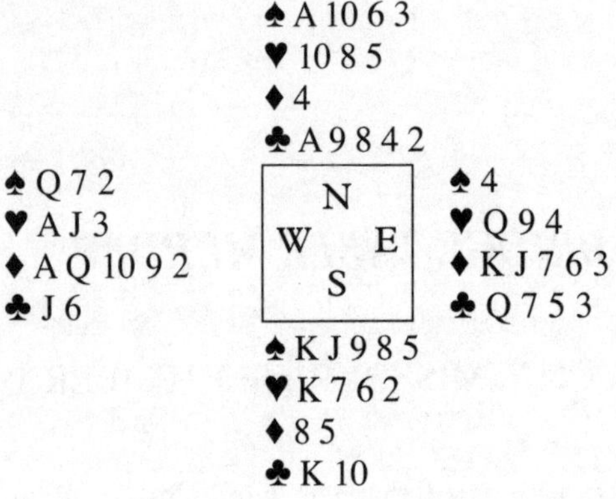

North: ♠A 10 6 3 ♥10 8 5 ♦4 ♣A 9 8 4 2

West: ♠Q 7 2 ♥A J 3 ♦A Q 10 9 2 ♣J 6

East: ♠4 ♥Q 9 4 ♦K J 7 6 3 ♣Q 7 5 3

South: ♠K J 9 8 5 ♥K 7 6 2 ♦8 5 ♣K 10

West	**North**	**East**	**South**
Hoffman	*Mrs Bennett*	*Mrs Hoffman*	*Bennett*
			1♠
2♦	4♠	All Pass	

Charles Hoffman led ♦A. Myrtle Bennett laid down her dummy and then retired to the kitchen to prepare for the next morning's breakfast.

Did John Bennett thank his wife? I do not know, but Mrs Hoffman later described the dummy as 'a good hand' and experts later claimed that her bid of Four Spades could not be criticised. But what about John Bennett's opener? Bennett had bid with ten points and a bit of shape, and his wife had expected a little more.

Having lost the first trick to ♦A and then faced a switch to ♣J on the second trick, Bennett had the problem of how to proceed. Experts would later point out that Four Spades was makable. Unfortunately, by the time experts assessed the hand, John Bennett was dead after going down.

There were several potential strategies: (i) play two top clubs, ending in dummy, then trump a third club (covered by the queen) with the eight, which can be overruffed if wished; (ii) play ♠K and then finesse West's ♠Q; (iii) end-play West for a ruff-and-discard or heart lead.

One expert advised a finesse in clubs but not in spades, as the percentage play was for ♠Q to drop in two rounds. That is, cash ♣A and run ♣9 from dummy. Then, if not covered, ruff the losing diamond and end-play. Declarer is short of an entry in dummy unless the trumps break two–two. West was fairly marked as holding ♥A.

Bennett is believed to have gone down by not taking the trump finesse (or by taking it wrong) and then wasting two good clubs after setting them up and cutting himself off from dummy. Bennett lost four tricks (♦A, ♥A, ♠Q and ♥Q).

After the hand had been played everything went wrong, according to Mrs Hoffman in her evidence at the later trial.

'You overbid,' John Bennett accused his wife.

'You're a bum bridge player,' said Myrtle Bennett, and the argument escalated before John Bennett reached across the bridge table and slapped his wife in the face several times. Then he folded up the table.

'Nobody but a bum would hit a woman in the presence of friends,' said Myrtle Bennett.

'I'm going to spend the night at a hotel,' said John Bennett. 'And tomorrow I'm leaving town.'

John Bennett went to the bedroom to pack a suitcase. Myrtle Bennett went to her mother's bedroom to pack a loaded gun.

When Bennett saw the gun, he ran to the bathroom and locked the door behind him. His wife fired twice. The shots missed. Bennett darted out of the bathroom by another door and fled for the apartment's front door. He never made it. His wife shot him twice and he staggered to a chair to utter his last words – 'She got me' – and then collapsed dead.

Well, that is one story.

When Myrtle Bennett was charged with first-degree murder, another story was told at the trial (seventeen months later) by her defence attorneys. It went something like this.

Mr and Mrs Bennett were like sweethearts and she would rather be dead than have caused the death of her husband. When John Bennett said he was leaving town, Myrtle Bennett dutifully went to get the pistol that her husband normally carried on out-of-town business trips. Unfortunately she stumbled into a chair and the pistol accidentally went off. The wounded John Bennett then tried to grab her arm to take the weapon, but the gun went off again, causing the fatal wound.

During the trial Myrtle Bennett 'is estimated to have shed more tears than Jane Cowl did in an entire season of *Common Clay*', according to one contemporary report, referring to a sensational soap opera of the day.

Ely Culbertson, editor of the *Bridge World*, was an expert witness at the trial. He said,

> We have heard of lives depending on the play of a card. It is not often that we find that figure of speech literally true. Here is a case in point. Mr Bennett had overbid his hand. Of that there can be no doubt, but even with this, so kind were the gods of distribution that he might have saved his life had he played his cards a little better. Mr Hoffman opened the diamond ace, then shifted to the club suit when he saw the dummy void of diamonds, and led the club knave. This Mr Bennett won with his king and started to pull the adverse trumps. Here again he flirted with death, as people so frequently do when they fail to have a plan either in the game of bridge or the game of life. He still could make his contract and save his life. The proper play before drawing the trumps would have been to establish the club suit, after ruffing the last diamond in the closed hand, upon which to discard losers in his own hand. Suppose Mr Bennett, when he took the club trick with his king, had led his last diamond and trumped it with one of dummy's small trumps. He could then lead a trump and go up with the king. ...Now he would lead the club ten, and, when Mr Hoffman followed suit, his troubles would be over. He would play the ace of clubs and lead the nine or eight. If Mrs Hoffman put up the queen, Mr Bennett should trump and let Mr Hoffman over-trump if he pleased. If Mr Hoffman, after winning his trick, led a heart, the contract and a life would be saved. If he led a diamond the same would be true. A lead of the trump might still have permitted the fatal dénoument but at least Mr Bennett

would have had the satisfaction of knowing that he had played the cards dealt him by fate to the very best of his ability.

The jury decided the death was accidental and Myrtle Bennett was acquitted. The jury was out for eight hours and three jurors tried to learn how to play bridge. Had four mastered the game, we can assume the jury would have been out for several days.

The background to the verdict was explained by a juror: 'She was only a woman, unused to guns. We reckoned that if she'd really been trying to hit him she would have missed.' And so Mrs Bennett was able to collect on an insurance policy worth $30,000 (£6,150).

One outcome was a sick joke – shooting a bad bridge partner is justifiable homicide – but a better anecdote came from Alexander Woollcott, when he followed up Mrs Bennett a few years later: 'She has not allowed her bridge to grow rusty, even though she occasionally encounters an inexplicable difficulty in finding a partner. Recently she took on one unacquainted with history. Having made an impulsive bid, he put his hand down with some diffidence. "Partner," he said, "I'm afraid you'll want to shoot me for this." Mrs Bennett, says my informant, had the good grace to faint.'

PERFECT HANDS

LONDON, OCTOBER 1929

This hand was dealt at the Carlton Hotel and the cards had supposedly been shuffled six or seven times before they were passed to George du Cros, the dealer. When du Cros saw his hand – thirteen diamonds – he immediately laid it down on the table.

'What can you do about this?' he asked.

'Keep your cards up,' said Sir Charles Sykes, who knew he had the winning hand.

Dealer East.

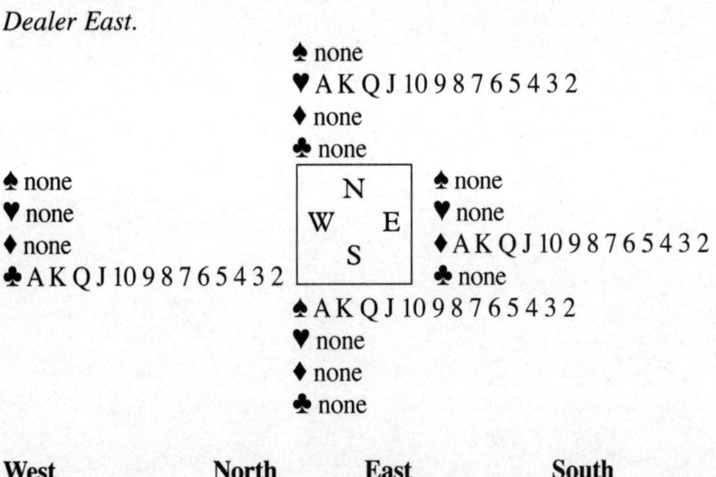

West	**North**	**East**	**South**
Sir C Mandelberg	*A G Rossiter*	*George du Cros*	*Sir Charles Sykes*
		7 ♦	7 ♠
All Pass			

This hand came only a month after one legendary Chicago game had produced a whole evening of perfect hands. One player, Alice Reidy, had supposedly held two of them – thirteen spades at one time and thirteen diamonds shortly after. Later the same evening she was dealt a hand containing twelve clubs and one heart.

Another player in the same Chicago game, Edna Newell, was dealt a perfect No-trump hand – four aces, four kings, four queens and ♠J – while an opponent held four twos, four threes, four fours and a five. This perfect No-trump hand seems very close to the kind that is easy to rig from a new pack of cards (see page 261).

A few years later a group of American statisticians, concerned about the high number of reported perfect hands, began monitoring their incidence. They estimated that there should be no more than two or three claims each year of a player being dealt thirteen cards of one suit. In the first monitored year, however, they discovered 52 cases of one-suiters, but 48 of these claimed a complete suit of spades and three claimed all hearts.

THIRTEEN HEARTS BUT SEVERAL DOWN

BOSWORTH, MISSOURI, DECEMBER 1929

Of all the early stories of perfect hands, perhaps the most surprising was that of Wes Stafford, a hardware dealer from the Midwest, who dealt himself thirteen hearts. Stafford had a quick glance at his cards and saw a lot of red. He bid One Diamond 'just to get the game started'. Everyone else passed.

By then Stafford had taken a closer look at his hand. The red cards were all hearts. Thirteen of them.

He laid the unplayed cards down on the table. The contract of One Diamond was untenable, even with dummy's help. 'The comment of Mrs Stafford, his partner, is not on record,' stated the *New York Times* (28 December 1929).

The Stafford story is reminiscent of an old tale about a Californian whist player who dealt himself thirteen hearts (making hearts trumps) and yet made only one trick. How come? Well, when he trumped his partner's ace on the first trick, his angry partner shot him.

THIRTEEN HEARTS AND OUTBID

COLORADO SPRINGS, COLORADO, MARCH 1930

Pity poor West on this hand. Thirteen hearts and no chance to bid to become declarer.

Dealer North.

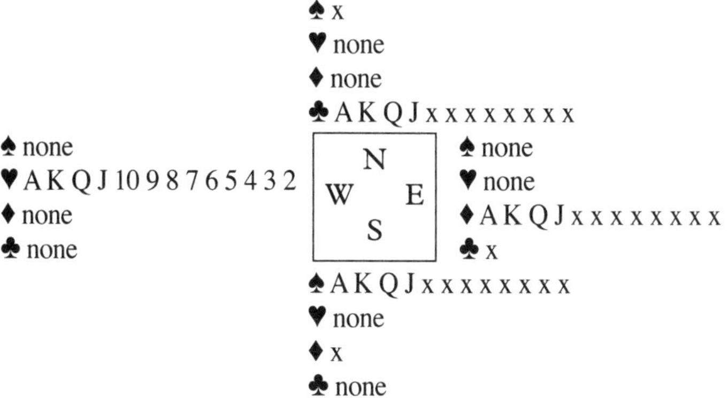

West	North	East	South
Mrs Arra Conway	*Mrs Anna Fleming*	*Mrs Borden*	*Mrs Ryan*
	6 ♣	6 ♦	6 ♠
7 ♥	Pass	Pass	7 ♠
All Pass			

THE PSYCHIC BID

USA, 1931

The term 'psychic bid' was first used by Dorothy Sims in the early 1920s, although people in Britain had referred to 'spoof bids' and 'bluff bids'. A psychic bid is one which describes your hand falsely in order to lure opponents into the wrong contract or making the wrong lead.

This hand is taken from Sims's classic book, *Psychic Bidding* (1932). The star North was Sir Derrick Wernher, who was British by birth but spent the 1920s and 1930s in the United States, where he played high-class bridge.

Dealer South. East–West Game.

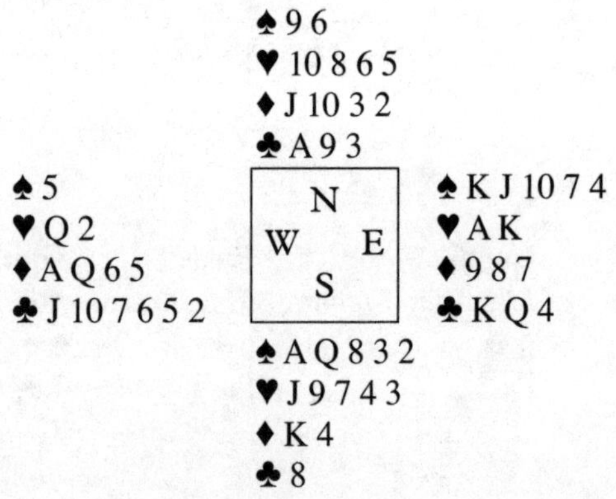

West	**North**	**East**	**South**
	Wernher		
			Pass
Pass	1 ♠	Dble	2 ♥
3 ♣	3 NT	Dble	4 ♠
Pass	Pass	Dble	Pass
Pass	5 ♥	Dble	All Pass

Wernher opened on five points because he suspected that East–West would find a successful game contract if East was allowed to open the bidding. Wernher's partner bid hearts, intending to switch to spades later. Wernher then anticipated that East–West would find a contract of Three No-trumps on East's next bid. If so, declarer would probably have little trouble, although the location of the spades might be a surprise. So Wernher bid Three No-trumps himself.

East was now stuck. He doubled. Then South unexpectedly bid Four Spades. After East again doubled, Wernher retreated into Five Hearts. That contract was two away for a loss of 200 points (on the scoring of the day). And Three No-trumps by East–West would indeed make.

Sims's book also includes the case of the man who opened One No-trump on a yarborough with nothing above a six. The opposition reached Six Spades anyway, and the man sitting opposite the yarborough doubled with twelve points. Declarer redoubled and made all thirteen tricks. A reminder that psychic bidders may have to pay more on their insurance policies.

THE BRIDGE BATTLE OF THE CENTURY

NEW YORK CITY, DECEMBER 1931 TO JANUARY 1932

This challenge match, between teams captained by Ely Culbertson and Sidney Lenz, did much to popularise bridge in the 1930s. 'The match was played in a glare of publicity such as never has attended any other bridge game nor ever will again,' said Terence Reese and David Bird in *Famous Hands from Famous Matches* (1991). 'The day-by-day scores were front-page news in 30 countries and every move was reported on the radio.'

The challenge involved personalities and bidding systems. The flamboyant Culbertson had already successfully matched his approach-forcing system against the English system (or lack of system) of Lieutenant-Colonel Buller. Although Buller called his opponent's system the Cumbersome System, a sporting 200-hand match ended with the Culbertson team convincing winners by 4,865 points.

Culbertson published his system in *The Blue Book*, promoted it through his magazine, the *Bridge World*, and made himself a well-known brand name. To extend his popularity, Culbertson felt he needed to take on a team from a rival American organisation, Bridge Headquarters, to prove that his system was better than the 'official system'. The challenge was issued and eventually taken up.

Culbertson and his wife, Josephine, promoted themselves as the young, loving married couple taking on jealous authorities. Indeed, there was an subliminal sexual undercurrent to Culbertson's system, and he made no secret of it: 'The game brought men and women together, and I used phrases like forcing bid and approach bid because they had a connotation of sex.'

The first of 150 rubbers in the Culbertson–Lenz match was played on Monday 7 December and the match continued on four evenings a week. The standard of the bridge was not particularly high, but the hands provoked discussion throughout the nation. The Lenz team took an early lead, but by the sixth session there was little between the two sides. In the eighth session came one of the most famous hands of the match.

Dealer South. Game All.

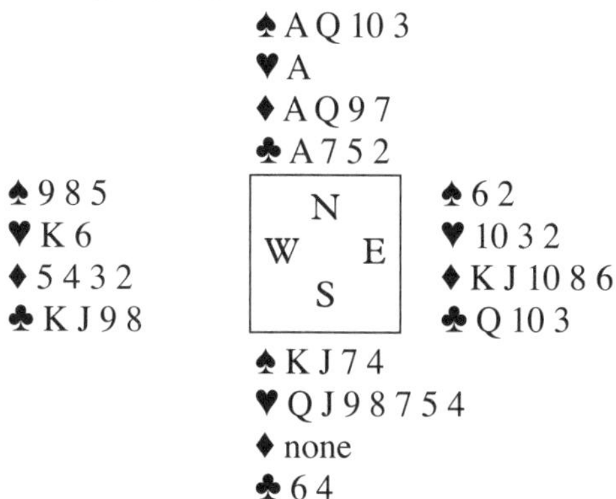

West	**North**	**East**	**South**
Ely Culbertson	*Lenz*	*Lightner*	*Jacoby*
			1 ♥
Pass	3 NT	Pass	4 ♥
Pass	4 NT	Pass	5 ♥
Pass	6 NT	Pass	Pass
Dble	Pass	Pass	7 ♥
Dble	All Pass		

After a competition between Jacoby and Lenz, the latter looked to have secured the hand with his favoured No-trumps. At this point Culbertson cheekily doubled and then doubled again when Jacoby tried to escape into Seven Hearts. The contract went one down.

Jacoby was criticised for his light opening bid, and Lenz was criticised for continually bidding No-trumps, as he did during the whole match.

Here is Jacoby's later commentary: 'Although I did not hold two and a half or even two quick tricks, I was nevertheless prepared to play the hand at Four Hearts, even if my partner held very little. In fact, I might well have bid Four Hearts on this hand originally, were it not that my second suit was spades, and I did not want to shut out a possible spade bid by my partner.'

The ideal contract was Seven Spades, but Six No-trumps would have made unless Lightner had led a club.

The Culbertson team eventually won the match by 8,950 points.

THE FIRST WORLD PAR OLYMPIAD

AROUND THE WORLD, APRIL 1932

The original idea was for a million players around the world to play sixteen hands prepared by Ely and Jo Culbertson. As Ely Culbertson wrote in the *Bridge World* (June 1931):

> At the chosen hour, in every city of the world, those entering the contest will be given the hands in specially designed boards. These hands will be so arranged that the players sitting North and South and East and West will have equal opportunity to display their skill in bidding and their accuracy in play... Through this competition a dream of civilisation will be realised. At one particular hour and extending for several hours, people of all races and languages will be speaking the one universal language – of bridge.

The event, originally scheduled for January, was delayed until April. The starting time (8 p.m. New York time) put off many British people, including the editor of *Bridge Magazine*: 'My enthusiasm for the Million Players Championship...has been somewhat damped by the announcement that in order to synchronise with New York time, competitors in England will have to start play at the hour of one o'clock in the morning.'

Culbertson's biographer, John Clay, documents how Culbertson met with setbacks when the Olympic Games Committee complained about the use of the term 'Olympiad' and when details of the hands were leaked. Culbertson did not achieve his goal of a million players. However, the par contest stayed in the bridge calendar and its record participation came in 1934, when 90,000 players took part in over 70 countries.

In the first Bridge Olympiad, the sixteenth hand was included as light relief after the strain of the first fifteen hands. It was based on a goulash deal, and West was not allowed to open the bidding with Seven Hearts. Here is the most curious example of the bidding.

Dealer South. East–West Game.

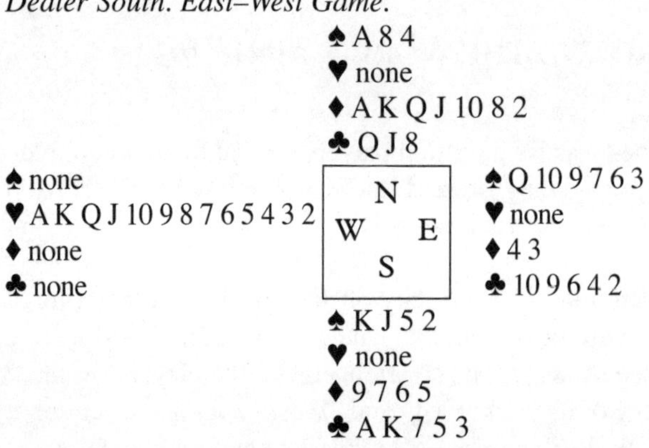

West	**North**	**East**	**South**
			1 ♣
1 ♦ (i)	2 ♥ (ii)	All Pass (iii)	

(i) A psychic
(ii) Another psychic (realising West's bid was a psychic)
(iii) West was certain that North's bid was a psychic

The contract was eight down when West claimed all thirteen tricks. Here is how the Culbertsons scored the hand:

East–West par: any score playing the hand at hearts.
North–South par: Seven No-trumps bid and made in case West overcalls immediately with Seven Hearts. If West does not bid Seven Hearts immediately, par for North–South is Seven Hearts doubled and made by opponents.

THE SCHWAB TROPHY

LONDON, JULY 1933

Ely and Jo Culbertson took part in another grand challenge match in 1933, when they met a team captained by Lieutenant-Colonel 'Pops' Beasley in the Palm Court at Selfridges in Oxford Street. The Schwab Trophy was an attempt to create something for bridge akin to tennis's Davis Cup, but most European bridge officials scoffed at attempts to call the match an international.

'The match, for which the Schwab Cup was the pretext, between an American team led by Mr Culbertson and a team led by Lt.-Col. H. M. Beasley, could on no account be regarded as anything but a private match,' wrote N P Wakar in the French publication *La Revue du Bridge*.

The match consisted of 300 boards, duplicated in two rooms in a team-pairs format. It was another big media event. The hands were followed closely by spectators – with the help of an electrical scoreboard displaying the hands and a periscope to see the players in action – and there was plenty of incident away from the table too. One English player, Graham Mathieson, fell through a glass roof and was rescued hanging by one hand to an iron girder over a 40-foot drop.

The match was accompanied by a British heatwave, but Selfridges placed large blocks of ice in strategic places. The British team led by 1,170 points after the first day and increased their lead to 3,390 points after 112 boards, but the Americans fought back. Culbertson's team led by 7,970 points when it came to the sensational 232rd board.

Dealer East. North–South Game.

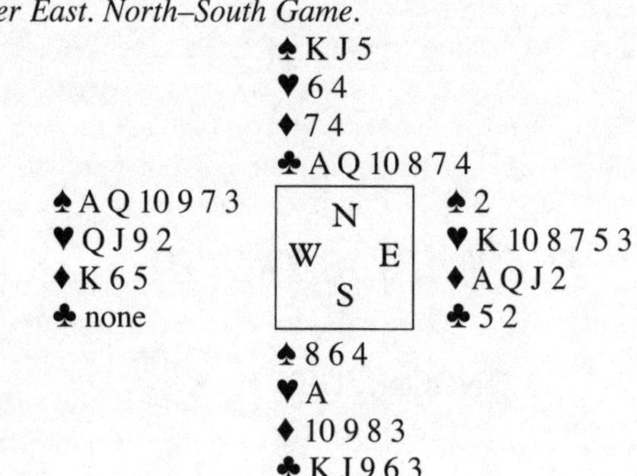

Room 1

West	**North**	**East**	**South**
Morris	*Jo Culbertson*	*Tabbush*	*Gottlieb*
		Pass	Pass
1 ♠	Pass	3 ♥	Pass
5 ♥	Pass	6 ♥	All Pass

Room 2

West	**North**	**East**	**South**
Culbertson	*Beasley*	*Lightner*	*Domville*
		1 ♥	Pass
1 ♠	2 ♣	Pass	2 ♥
All Pass			

Beasley's pair made twelve tricks in Room 1 for 980 points. In Room 2, Sir Henry Domville's bid of Two Hearts was an attempt to show that he had first-round control in the suit. Beasley assumed the bid was genuine because Domville had not overcalled Two Hearts on the first round of bidding. Beasley later conceded that he should have bid again anyway.

As he wrote later:

> This hand resulted in one of the most comical disasters of the match, and both Domville and myself had several frenzied telephone inquiries next morning from Shanghai and Timbuctoo.

When I heard Domville's Two Heart bid – mark you, he had already passed – I had to guess one of two things, either Lightner had opened on a short heart suit and Domville had something like seven to the queen, knave, ten, and the ace of diamonds, or else he had no hearts and did not want me to be put off bidding a game in clubs if Culbertson's bid was a semi-psychic.

The answer is that I should not have taken my guess then and there but should have made another bid to find out, when, if he had seven hearts, he could have rebid to three without much damage. His point of view had its merits but was rather confusing at the time for anybody to realise properly. I think he could have achieved more by bidding Two No-trumps.

Culbertson led ♥Q and the Americans won twelve tricks. Seven down vulnerable was worth 1,750 points in those days. (Undoubled vulnerable undertricks scored 100 for the first, 150 for the second, 200 for the third, 250 for the fourth and so on.)

The hand was a big embarrassment to Beasley's team. Reporters joked that Domville's heart bids showed he either had hearts or he didn't.

The Englishmen lost 770 points on the board, and Culbertson's team eventually won by 104,080 points to the Beasley team's 93,180. The following year the Americans returned to win the Schwab Trophy by 3,600 points.

THE NULLO

USA, 1934

Just as solo whist has its bid of *misère*, where the aim is not to win a trick, so bridge has had its nullo option. The nullo was another 'suit' between spades and no-trumps. To bid nullo was to say how many tricks you were *not* going to make.

The nullo was first introduced around 1917 as a means of entertaining players who held bad cards and it played a part in auction bridge in the 1920s. In *Bridge Magazine* (January 1935), R F Foster called for its return: 'Today we have the same outcry against the invincible big slam hands that compel two players to sit still and allow their adversaries to score perhaps anywhere from 2,890 to 3,340 points simply by laying down their cards to show the inevitable.'

In practice, however, players found it difficult to learn the mentality of *losing* tricks. The nullo was not officially adopted in the laws, but players agreed to its use in some matches.

A bridge magazine writer described an evening of nullos as follows:

> The muddle was magnificent. One partner, with a lovely-looking yarborough, would smile delightedly and start off with about 'Five Nullos', while the other partner had a most enormous hand of honours, and had to try to take her *out* or *in* (I don't know quite which) into a slam that they could not possibly make. We had one success, where things really came off. My partner and I, both with hopeless hands, called a Grand Slam in Nullos (no tricks) and we made it – or didn't make it – against the other two, who held the earth and were wild.

Here is an example:

Dealer West. East–West Game.

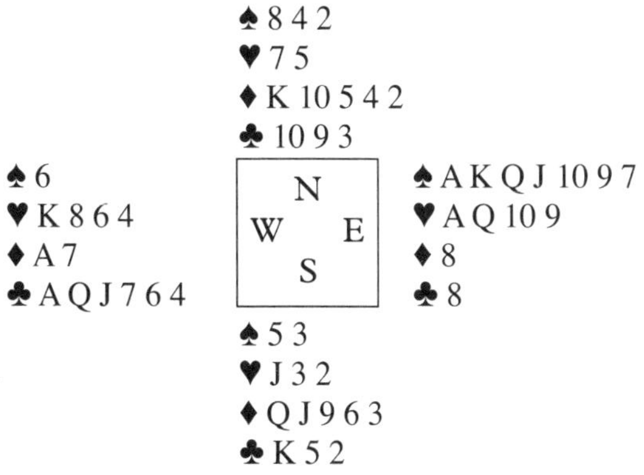

Room 1

West	**North**	**East**	**South**
1 ♣	Pass	2 ♠	Pass
3 ♣	Pass	3 ♠	Pass
3 NT	Pass	4 NT	Pass
5 NT	Pass	7 ♠	7 Nullos
All Pass			

Without any rules of what to lead against Seven Nullos, West opted for ♣A. Declarer played dummy's nine and king from hand. West then led ♣7 and declarer won with the ten. East was able to discard ♥A.

West won declarer's club continuation, East discarding ♥Q, and then led ♥4 to East's ten. When East returned his last heart, West could take it with the king and lead another heart to the jack in declarer's hand.

Two away.

In the other room, East bid to Six Spades and North–South sacrificed in Six Nullos. The defence was poor and declarer was able to make only one trick (or *not make* twelve tricks). That is, declarer made Six Nullos.

You may have noticed that East–West could have made Seven No-trumps, a higher-ranking bid than Seven Nullos.

BANNED BY THE POLICE

HARROGATE, MARCH 1934

The British Bridge League planned their inaugural congress for the Majestic Hotel, Harrogate, but the police intervened and the congress was abandoned. The laws of the day permitted local authorities to ban games on licensed premises.

In the 1930s, there was no reason (other than common sense) why the police should not ban every bridge congress. Most card games were illegal under a statute dating back to the reign of Henry VIII, who had outlawed any game that might interfere with archery practice. The issue was not whether bridge was a game of chance or skill, but where – or even if – any game was permitted to take place.

A replacement congress was hurriedly arranged for Eastbourne, where the authorities were more amenable, and participants were assured that they would be breaking no laws. The *Eastbourne Gazette* summarised:

> Everybody knows, for instance, that the licensing laws and the gaming laws of this country are in a state of unintelligible chaos, and most people agree that until they can be swept away or adapted to present-day conditions the better course is to forget them. It seems to us that to apply the gaming laws to a bridge congress is as ridiculous as it would be to enforce the ancient laws on Sabbath observation by prosecuting all visitors who do not attend church on Sundays.

Right on cue, certain members of the clergy objected to bridge taking place on a Sunday afternoon and Sunday evening in Eastbourne. The congress organisers responded by saying that they had kept Sunday morning free for church attendance, and certain players pointed out that they knew parsons, priests and bishops who themselves played bridge on Sunday evenings. Eventually the 468-hand Eastbourne Congress, held in April 1934, was deemed to be a success.

The Harrogate authorities grudgingly allowed a congress to take place the following year, but bridge organisers had more trouble ahead. In the late 1930s, some bridge clubs were prosecuted for having fruit machines on the premises. The errant clubs were fined and their machines were destroyed.

Alfred Manning-Foster stated the case in an editorial of *Bridge Magazine* (June 1939):

> Although there is nothing disreputable in having these machines in clubs, and most of us may think their suppression silly, we cannot get away from the fact that they are definitely illegal. It does not do a club any good to be raided and I hope that all bridge clubs which value their good name and reputation, will take prompt steps in the matter.

In the period up to the amendment of Henry VIII's statute, in 1945, bridge players continued to be under threat, but poker players were the more likely to be arrested. There was another spot of bother in 1970, when a charity bridge tournament attracted nearly 500 members of London society to Claridge's Hotel. The charge was five guineas per table and some players gambled for low stakes. Unfortunately, the 1968 Gaming Act prohibited gambling except on registered or licensed premises.

Most bridge clubs now operate on the right side of the law, but that does not keep the police away. They may arrive to inform a player about a crime or a death in the family, or they may be called to break up a fight between partners who have fallen out in a bad way. Then again they may be there already – some of them are very good players.

STEALING OPPONENTS' SLAM BIDS (1)

STOCKHOLM, SWEDEN, 1936

Vienna-born Hans Jellinek was one of the great bridge players of the 1930s. His partnership with Karl Schneider helped Austria to become European champions in 1936 and world champions the following year. In both championships Jellinek bid and played a small slam in opponents' strongest suit – the first time with a two–one trump fit, the second time with a zero–two fit – and each time the outcome was favourable to the Austrian team. The first occasion was when Austria played Sweden in the 1936 European Championships.

Dealer West. East–West Game.

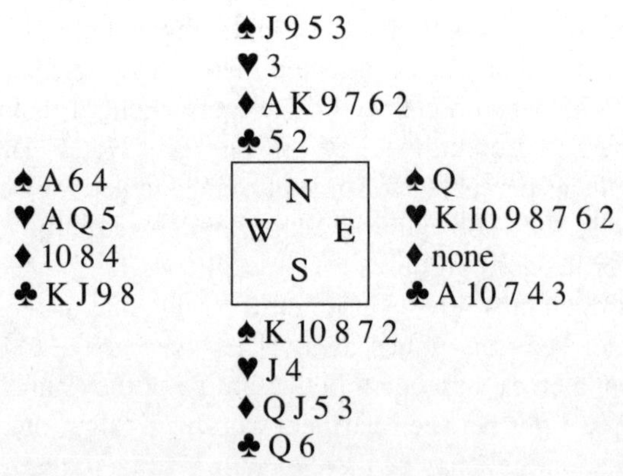

West	**North**	**East**	**South**
	Schneider		*Jellinek*
1 ♣	1 ♦	1 ♥	1 ♠
2 ♥	Pass	3 ♦	3 ♥
3 ♠	4 ♣	6 ♣	6 ♥
All Pass			

The bidding was orderly enough until East cue-bid diamonds to explore slam possibilities. Then Jellinek bid Three Hearts to ask for a heart lead against clubs. This was the first ruse. After West had cue-bid Three Spades to show first-round spade control, Schneider falsely cue-bid clubs as if asking for a club lead against hearts. When East bid Six Clubs, Jellinek prevented West from bidding Six Hearts *by bidding it himself.*

According to Norman Hart in *The Bridge Players' Bedside Book* (1939), Jellinek 'had a curiously clever method of inhibiting a grand slam impending against him by himself bidding the small slam in the opponent's suit. He did this when it seemed clear that the bidding of the small slam was going to be for his opponents an essential step in reaching the grand slam.'

West had wanted to bid Six Hearts to encourage East to go to seven. Now, with no idea that East–West could make Seven Clubs or Seven Hearts (with only 23 points), West attempted a forcing pass.

East was not sure which of his opponents' bids were genuine and which were psychic. Judging by the odd shape of his own hand, he was willing to believe that North might have a club void and South might have a heart void. Also, a double might force his opponents to take refuge in Seven Spades or Seven Diamonds. Better to take a larger penalty by defending Six Hearts undoubled. So East passed. Hans Jellinek went twelve down to concede 600 points.

In the other room the Austrians bid to Seven Hearts and North–South sacrificed in Seven Spades (doubled). It was still a good sacrifice, as Seven Hearts would make for 2,960 points. Instead, Sweden lost 1,000 points for five down (doubled) and Austria gained 400 on the board.

STEALING OPPONENTS' SLAM BIDS (2)

BUDAPEST, HUNGARY, JUNE 1937

Hans Jellinek did it again in an early round of the World Championships. This time he and his partner were vulnerable, and the vulnerable grand-slam bonus had been reduced from 2,250 to 1,500 points, but the sacrifice was still worthwhile.

Dealer West. Game All.

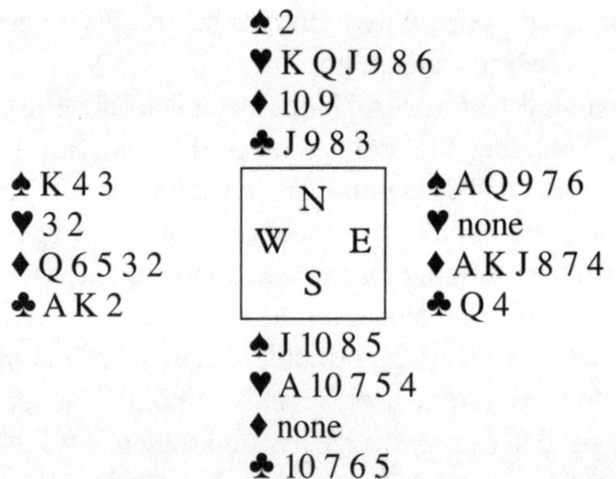

♠ 2
♥ K Q J 9 8 6
♦ 10 9
♣ J 9 8 3

♠ K 4 3
♥ 3 2
♦ Q 6 5 3 2
♣ A K 2

♠ A Q 9 7 6
♥ none
♦ A K J 8 7 4
♣ Q 4

♠ J 10 8 5
♥ A 10 7 5 4
♦ none
♣ 10 7 6 5

West	North	East	South
	Schneider		*Jellinek*
1 ♦	1 ♥	2 ♥	3 ♥
Pass	Pass	3 ♠	Pass
4 ♠	Pass	4 NT (i)	Pass
5 ♣ (ii)	Pass	5 ♦ (iii)	6 ♦ (iv)
All Pass (v)			

(i) Conventional (three aces or two aces plus king of genuinely bid suit)
(ii) Ace of clubs
(iii) This bid, rather than Six Diamonds, is probably asking partner either to choose between six or seven or to cue-bid some more
(iv) Jellinek spots that the opposition have Seven Diamonds on, so he takes the chance to introduce his tactic, looking to save in Six Hearts if he is doubled
(v) West is not confident enough to bid Seven Diamonds on his holding, and Six Spades might be risky if East holds only four spades; doubling would result in opponents bidding hearts

Once more Jellinek lost all thirteen tricks, this time at a cost of 1,200 points. Six Hearts (doubled) would have been down three tricks, losing three clubs and a spade, so East–West could be justified in passing rather than doubling. In the other room the Austrians bid and made Seven Diamonds for 2,140 points. The swing to the Austrians was 940 points.

Hans Jellinek emigrated to Norway at the beginning of the Second World War, but the Norwegian government under Quisling provided no sanctuary for Jewish people. Jellinek was deported in 1940 and died in Auschwitz.

AUSTRIA VS. CULBERTSON (1)

BUDAPEST, HUNGARY, JUNE 1937

The first-ever World Championships involved fifteen European teams, Egypt and two American teams – one from Minneapolis, captained by E Burns, and one from New York, captained by the inimitable Ely Culbertson. The Culbertson team scraped through a quarter-final with Norway on extra boards – after 72 hands, the points margin was less than the 300 required for a win – and went on to play the 96-board final against Austria.

After thirty boards the Austrians led by 1,140 points, and then the Culbertson team won back 400 points in the next twelve hands. By the end, however, the Austrians were convincing winners by 4,750 points.

The difference lay in the slam-bidding, where the Austrians gained 4,880 points. Dr Paul Stern's Austrian team bid and made five grand slams. They also bid and made five small slams. Their only two failures in the slam zone were one small-slam bid that went off and one slam attempt that cost them a game. One expert thought the difference between the Austrians and the Americans was that the Austrians used asking bids better and generally showed more natural flair.

See what you make of the natural flair on Board 23, which arrived when Austria led by 180 points. Perhaps it is not the best example.

Dealer South. North–South Game.

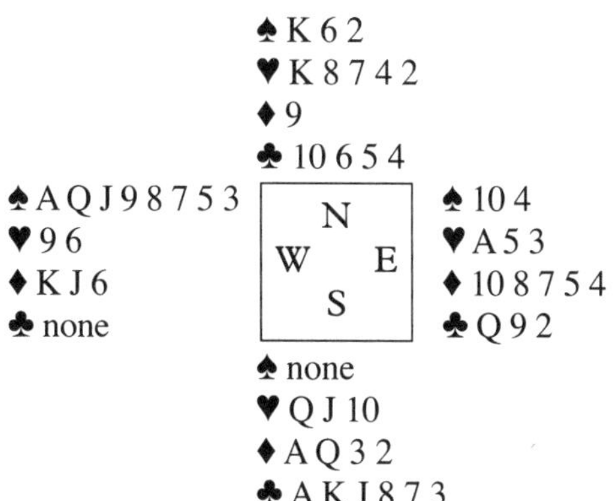

♠ K 6 2
♥ K 8 7 4 2
♦ 9
♣ 10 6 5 4

West		East
♠ A Q J 9 8 7 5 3		♠ 10 4
♥ 9 6		♥ A 5 3
♦ K J 6		♦ 10 8 7 5 4
♣ none		♣ Q 9 2

♠ none
♥ Q J 10
♦ A Q 3 2
♣ A K J 8 7 3

Room 1

West	**North**	**East**	**South**
Helen Sobel	*Jellinek*	*Vogelhofer*	*Schneider*
			1 ♣
4 ♠	Pass	Pass	5 ♠ (i)
Pass	5 NT (ii)	Pass	6 ♣
All Pass			

(i) Schneider meant to bid Five Clubs on the second round but he made a 'linguistic error' and the suit came out wrong
(ii) Jellinek knew that he must not pass Five Spades but he thought Six Clubs would be too high

Room 2

West	**North**	**East**	**South**
Von Blühdorn	*Jo Culbertson*	*Herbert*	*Ely Culbertson*
			1 ♣
4 ♠	Dble	All Pass	

In Room 1, Schneider made his dubious contract (from 23 high-card points) and Austria scored 1,370 points.

In the other room, West's Four Spades went one off for 100 points. The swing to Austria of 1,270 points gave Austria a lead of 1,450 in the match.

AUSTRIA VS. CULBERTSON (2)

BUDAPEST, HUNGARY, JUNE 1937

Culbertson's American team trailed the Austrians by 890 points at the start of the last sixteen-hand session of the World Championships final. Here, on Board 81, the Austrians certainly showed 'natural flair' as they bid to Grand Slam while the Americans stopped in game.

Dealer South. East–West Game.

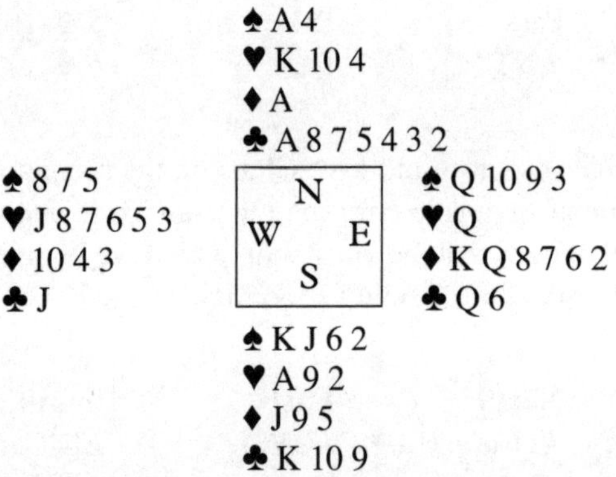

Room 1

West	**North**	**East**	**South**
Helen Sobel	*Frischauer*	*Vogelhofer*	*Herbert*
			1 ♣
Pass	1 NT	Pass	2 NT
Pass	3 ♣	Pass	3 ♠
Pass	4 ♣	Pass	5 ♣
Pass	7 ♣	All Pass	

Room 2

West	**North**	**East**	**South**
Jellinek	*Jo Culbertson*	*Schneider*	*Ely Culbertson*
			Pass
Pass	1 ♣	Pass	1 ♠
Pass	2 ♣	Pass	2 NT
Pass	3 NT	All Pass	

The Austrians made all thirteen tricks in Room 1 (for 1,440 points), Herbert choosing the heart finesse, but the Culbertsons' thirteen tricks in Room 2 were worth only 520 points. Austria's lead grew to 1,810 points.

AUSTRIA VS. CULBERTSON (3)

BUDAPEST, HUNGARY, JUNE 1937

As the margin between the two teams in the World Championships final grew larger, Culbertson's team lost further points when trying to bid back into contention. The penultimate board of the match, Board 95, was one of the last hands that Ely and Jo Culbertson played together.

Dealer South. Love All.

	North	
	♠K 9 4 3 ♥A 9 ♦A 10 9 5 4 3 2 ♣none	
West ♠8 ♥K Q 6 2 ♦K 8 7 ♣Q J 4 3 2	N / W E / S	**East** ♠Q 5 ♥J 10 7 4 ♦Q J ♣K 10 9 7 5
	♠A J 10 7 6 2 ♥8 5 3 ♦6 ♣A 8 6	

Room 1

West	North	East	South
Vogelhofer	*Herbert*	*Helen Sobel*	*Frischauer*
			1 ♠
Pass	2 ♦	Pass	2 ♠
Pass	4 ♥ (i)	Pass	4 ♠ (ii)
Pass	5 ♦ (iii)	Pass	5 NT (iv)
Pass	7 ♠	All Pass	

(i) Agreeing spades and asking for a second-round control in hearts
(ii) Denying a heart control
(iii) Asking for a second-round diamond control
(iv) Showing second-round diamond control and two aces

Room 2

West	**North**	**East**	**South**
Schneider	Ely Culbertson	Jellinek	Jo Culbertson
			1 ♠
Pass	2 ♦	Pass	2 ♠
Pass	4 ♥	Pass	4 ♠
Pass	5 ♦	All Pass	

Seven Spades from twenty high-card points made easily enough (1,510 points) and Five Diamonds just made (400 points). The debate centred on Jo Culbertson's failure to recognise that Five Diamonds was an asking bid.

As Paul Stern wrote in *Beating the Culbertsons* (1938):

> Mrs Culbertson, who did not seem quite at home in the asking bid, took this to mean that Culbertson wished to play the hand in Five Diamonds; and, under this delusion, passed. She had obviously not realised Culbertson's purpose in first calling Four Hearts. Mrs Culbertson may also have been anxious, on account of her weak opening bid, to sign off as quickly as possible. This lamentable misunderstanding cost America 1,100 points.

The match was virtually over at this point, and a hand later Austria won by 4,750.

Twelve years later Ben Cohen gave this same hand to four international players in Yorkshire. This is how they bid it.

West	**North**	**East**	**South**
			1 ♠
Dble (i)	3 ♦ (ii)	3 ♥	Pass
Pass	4 ♠	5 ♣	Pass
Pass	5 ♠	All Pass	

(i) Distributional double
(ii) Forcing for one round

What was new here was a little bit of competition. I guess one might expect that from twenty–twenty hands.

FIVE-SUIT BRIDGE

AROUND THE WORLD, 1937

'The game of five-suit bridge has aroused the interest of bridge players throughout the world,' wrote Samuel Fry and Edward Hymes in *How to Win at Five Suit Bridge* (1938). 'Five-suit bridge, in short, is governed by the same rules of play as contract bridge, except that this fifth suit is in it.'

Five-suit bridge was devised and patented by Dr Walter Marseille, a Viennese psychologist and mathematician. It was introduced in 1937 and played with a 65-card pack. Each player was dealt sixteen cards and the remaining card ('the widow') was placed face-upwards on the table.

The fifth suit was either green or blue in colour. It was known as 'leaves' in Austria, 'eagles' in America and 'royals' or 'crowns' in England. (The first chapter of the Fry and Hymes book was entitled 'Enter the Royals'.) After the bidding, declarer was allowed to replace one card with the widow card from the table. The discarded card was seen by all the other players.

The 'book' was eight tricks rather than six and the scoring was revised as the game evolved. In its more developed form, a game required 150 points and contracted tricks scored 30 for minors and majors, 40 for royals ('the super-major') and 50 for No-trumps. Eventually, slams scored 500 (non-vulnerable fifteen-trick Small Slam), 1,000 (vulnerable Small Slam and non-vulnerable sixteen-trick Grand Slam) or 2,000 (vulnerable Grand Slam).

Some people thought that five-suit bridge had fewer contracts of Three No-trumps than the four-suit game because it was harder to guard five suits. Others thought that Three No-trumps was easier with five suits because declarer could afford to lose five tricks in an unguarded suit. Fry and Hymes felt that misfit hands were safer in No-trumps in the five-suit variant. They had lots of tips, such as, 'Don't let two five-card suits go to your head.'

For a brief time in the late 1930s, there was a chance that the 65-card game might take over from 52-card bridge, but in the end this didn't happen. The *Western Mail* summed up the general feeling: 'I can see little hope of this new game ever taking the place of contract. For experts there may be additional scope in playing with a pack of 65 cards, but for most people the concentration needed to remember the extra 12 cards actually used is certain to prove beyond them.'

Fry and Hymes came up with one wonderful argument for the five-suit game:

> Just imagine the player who is addicted to weak overcalls. The opponents bid a spade and he overcalls with Two Clubs, which is promptly doubled. He now starts running, but when he has tried out Two Diamonds, Two Hearts, Two Spades and Two No-trumps, being doubled at all way-stations, he has no place left to go. Think of the orgy he can have at five-suit bridge. He may still end up going down plenty, but he will at least have one more chance to find a haven of refuge.

A correspondent for *The Times* plaintively asked what else might be changed. Would we have six-stump cricket, four-goal football, a twelve-oared Boat Race and eighteen-line sonnets?

Here is a specimen hand from the five-suit game:

Dealer West. North–South Game. Widow card ♠7.

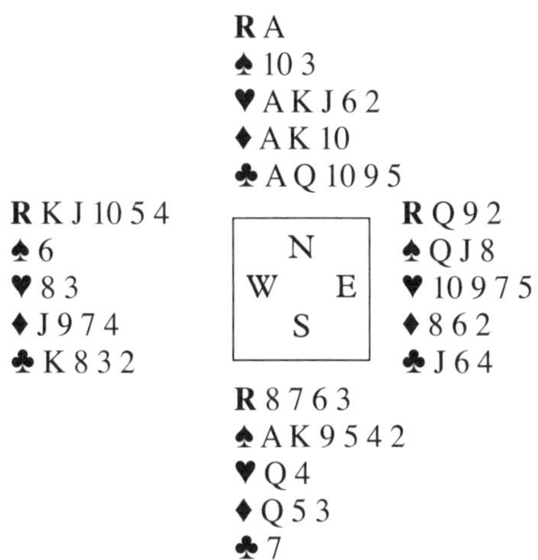

West	North	East	South
Pass	2 ♣	Pass	2 ♠
Pass	3 ♥	Pass	3 ♠
Pass	4 ♣	Pass	4 ♠
Pass	7 ♠	All Pass	

After the lead of a small royal, declarer exchanged the widow card (♠7) for one of dummy's clubs. This gave declarer three royal ruffs and only one loser (a spade). A cool 1,910 points at five-suit rubber bridge.

A famous five-suit bridge competition took place at Bournemouth in 1938, but the five-suit game did not survive the Second World War. There have been other attempts to adapt the pack. In the early 1960s, a new four-suit game used a 60-card pack, based on a book by Freddie Guest called *Fifteen: The Advanced Game of Contract Bridge* (1960). And, of course, one adaptation still available is midget bridge…

MIDGET BRIDGE

USA, 1937

If five-suit bridge was at one end of the continuum, then midget bridge was at the other. It was played with 36 cards and was enjoyed by people who had trouble shuffling, dealing and remembering a full pack of 52.

Cards lower than six were set aside and the remaining 36 dealt into four hands. Honours were not scored and the minor suits were worth the same as the majors (30 points). The 'book' was three tricks rather than six, and slams were scored for bids at the five and six levels. Bidding length was three of a suit rather than four. One advantage was that you could not go more than six down in a contract of Three No-trumps.

One evening I played a few hands of midget bridge. The first hand was a straightforward slam in clubs one way and a sensible five-spade sacrifice the other (one off). The third hand was an easy 24-point small slam, and the other two were game contracts. Two rubbers in about ten minutes.

Hand number six was a lay-down in Six No-trumps. In fact, the hand was so good that I was tempted to bid Seven No-trumps before I realised that that was an impossible contract. On the negative side, I saw one experienced bridge player revoke for the first time in her career.

Midget bridge probably has more entertainment value than five-suit bridge. For one thing it is easier to buy a suitable pack of cards.

Here is a little poser from a hand of midget bridge.

Dealer South.

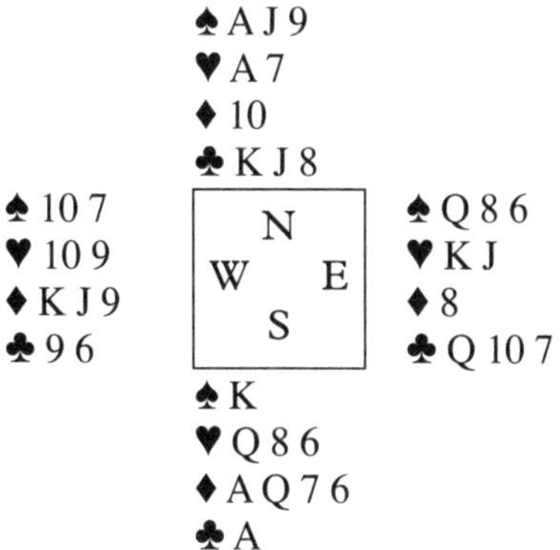

West	North	East	South
			1♦
Pass	1♠	Pass	2♥
Pass	5♥	All Pass	

The opening lead was ♠10. Can the small slam be made on any defence?

Declarer followed with ♠J from dummy and East guessed to play low. The singleton ♠K had to be played. Declarer cashed ♣A and ♦A and played a low heart to dummy's ace. A second heart from dummy forced East to win the trick and make an impossible lead – from ♣ Q 10 and ♠ Q 8 into dummy's ♣ K J and ♠ A 9. Whatever East led there were three tricks in dummy and the last trump in declarer's hand.

THE BENEFICIAL REVOKE

MANCHESTER, SEPTEMBER 1937

Modern bridge laws are very complex. The game has gone through a convoluted evolutionary process and at times the learning curve has been steep.

The scene is a rubber-bridge game near Manchester.

Dealer South. North–South Game.

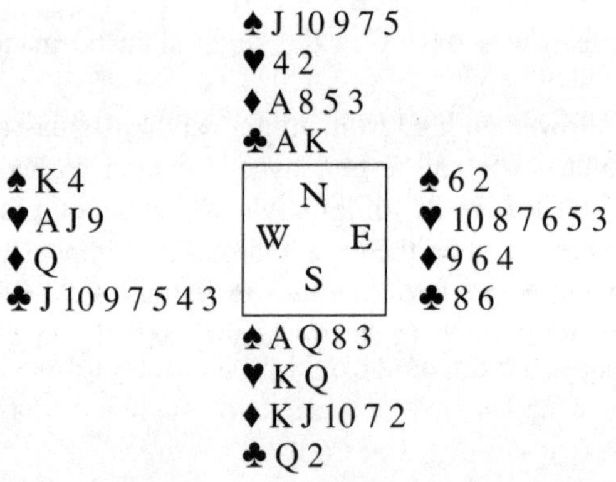

West	North	East	South
			1 NT
Pass	3 NT	Pass	Pass
Dble	All Pass		

West led ♣J, which was won by dummy's ace. Declarer then ran ♠J through to West's king. West led ♣3, which cleared the clubs and left West holding five winners.

Declarer returned to hand with the ♠A and led ♦J. When West discarded ♥9, declarer played ♦A from dummy and led ♦8. East played low, so declarer let the eight run. Imagine the surprise when West suddenly turned up with ♦Q.

West had obviously revoked on the first diamond.

South immediately drew attention to the revoke, everyone acknowledged it and West apologised profusely.

The law of the day, law 27(2) was clear: East–West would be penalised two tricks. Unfortunately, the law of the day was an ass.

Having got in under false pretences with ♦Q, West proceeded to cash five club winners and ♥A. That meant eight tricks for the defence, minus the penalty of two tricks. The contract was now two down, doubled and vulnerable, scoring 500 points for the defence.

Had West played properly, declarer would probably have made two club tricks, five diamonds and four spades for two over. That would have meant 200 points below the line, 400 points for overtricks and 700 for the two-game rubber.

The swing was 1,800 points in favour of the pair committing the offence. Justice?

That law had other anomalies. In the Manchester case the revoke had been noticed immediately, but what about a situation where the revoke was discovered at the end of the hand and declarer had shifted tactics during the play after assuming an unfavourable split?

Nowadays, an offending card can be returned to its correct position (but only if it is noticed immediately). The tournament director can also award sufficient tricks to cover the damage. If this case arose today, the director would probably award declarer nine tricks (or whatever seemed appropriate for the line of play).

THE LADIES BEAT THE GENTLEMEN

BIRMINGHAM, SEPTEMBER 1937

When women players like Josephine Culbertson and Dorothy Sims came to the public's attention, more women came into the game and there was plenty of scope for great challenge matches. A match between sixteen Warwickshire women and sixteen Warwickshire men was played on 30 September 1937. It may not rank alongside the Bobby Riggs vs. Billie Jean King tennis match as a battle of the sexes, but it was significant because the women beat the men by 2,340 points.

It is difficult to claim that the women were better overall, because one hand accounted for a swing of 4,810 points in their favour. Can you spot any gender differences in the bidding on this hand, or the number of tricks made?

Dealer East. North–South Game.

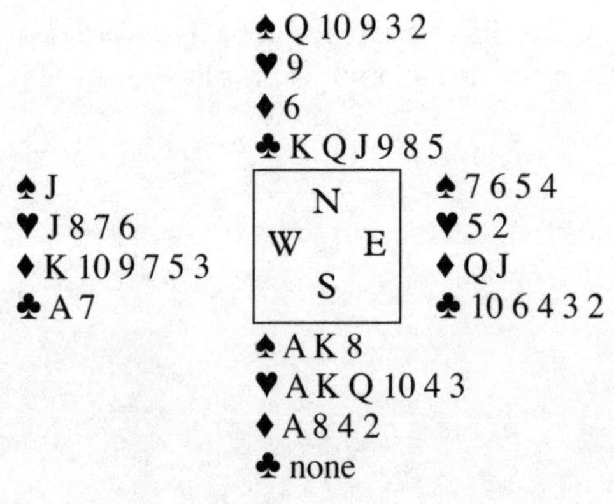

Contract	Declarer	Tricks	Women	Men
6 ♠	North (man)	11	100	
6 ♥ Redble	South (woman)	12	2,070	
6 ♥	South (man)	10	100	
6 ♥ Dble	South (woman)	12	1,710	
6 ♠	North (man)	11	100	
7 ♠ Dble	North (woman)	12		200
4 ♥	South (man)	12		780
6 ♥ Dble	South (woman)	12	1,710	

Bridge has seen many other male–female contests. The biggest came in April 1989, when more than 1,000 players took part in a battle of the sexes that was held simultaneously in Paris and New York City. For fifteen days, 24 hours a day, through 2,352 hands, women and men took up opposite seats in the two venues. The men won by 196 Individual Match Points (IMPs) – a very small margin for such a lengthy competition.

THE COMPLETE MISFIT

ENGLAND, NOVEMBER 1937

From January 1934, Angela wrote a regular column called 'Woman's Point of View' in *Bridge Magazine*. She wrote about clothes, cosmetics and cookery, and occasionally cards. Her theme was an evening's all-round entertainment. For instance, her Valentine's Day game needed eight 'sweeties' to draw partners from eight 'stalwarts' and heart contracts counted double (for or against).

Here is my favourite deal from Angela's columns. She claimed that this hand really happened. You may doubt the veracity of any hand containing eight voids, but it deserves its place here as a textbook example of the complete misfit.

Most bridge players experience the classic misfit at some stage. It is the hand where you feel you are competing with your partner rather than with the opposition. Afterwards your relationship with your partner may be just as big a misfit as the cards.

According to Angela, the bidding on this hand 'almost reads like a boxing commentary as there were so many rounds'. North and South used what author Spike Hughes once called 'the hammer-and-tongs system'. East and West waited patiently to double.

The ultimate misfit, however, comes when one player has thirteen spades and partner has thirteen clubs. On one occasion the latter bid Eight Clubs and the other bid Eight Spades.

Dealer South. North–South Game.

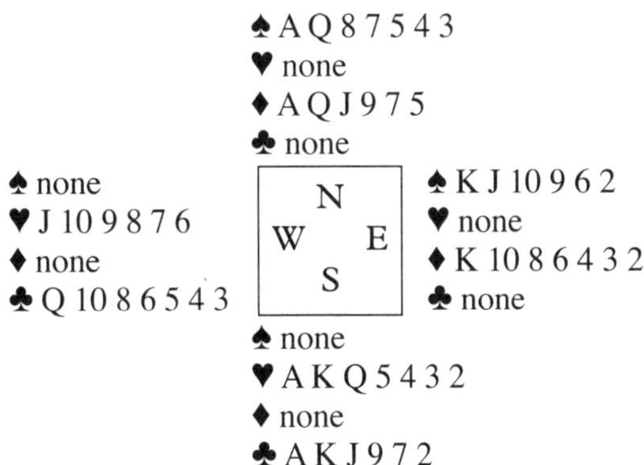

North:
♠ A Q 8 7 5 4 3
♥ none
♦ A Q J 9 7 5
♣ none

West:
♠ none
♥ J 10 9 8 7 6
♦ none
♣ Q 10 8 6 5 4 3

East:
♠ K J 10 9 6 2
♥ none
♦ K 10 8 6 4 3 2
♣ none

South:
♠ none
♥ A K Q 5 4 3 2
♦ none
♣ A K J 9 7 2

West	**North**	**East**	**South**
			2 ♥
Pass	2 ♠	Pass	3 ♣
Pass	3 ♦	Pass	3 ♥
Pass	3 ♠	Pass	4 ♣
Pass	4 ♦	Pass	4 ♥
Dble	4 ♠	Dble	5 ♥
Dble	All Pass		

Only two hands were actually involved in the play to any effect. South and West played a game within a game, and East did not even have an opportunity to revoke. East's cards could have been turned over and played at random.

The contract goes two or three down.

Prudence should have kept the bidding to three or four rounds rather than seven, but if you think 25 calls was an excessive amount of bidding, read on…

FOURTEEN ROUNDS OF BIDDING

ENGLAND, 1938

Every kitchen-bridge quartet is familiar with one common question: 'Could we have a recap of the bidding, please?' Usually someone at the table can respond with a quick summary. But what if there were fourteen rounds of bidding?

Norman Hart found this specimen for his *Daily Telegraph and Morning Post* column during the 1930s. He claimed it as a world record. I dare not do likewise – a lot of bidding has passed (or been passed) since – but a book of strange bridge hands needs one example of interminable bidding. Hart described it as 'an interesting curiosity'.

In the fourteen rounds there were twelve bids, eight doubles, three redoubles, and 32 passes. The auction took more than half an hour.

A club director would not be pleased to find a table engaged in bidding for 30 minutes, especially if the players were up and down from their seats while trying to borrow extra bidding cards. In fact, with normal ACOL bidding, the auction would be over in four rounds. It was the unravelling of psychic bids that took the bidding space.

Dealer West. North–South Game.

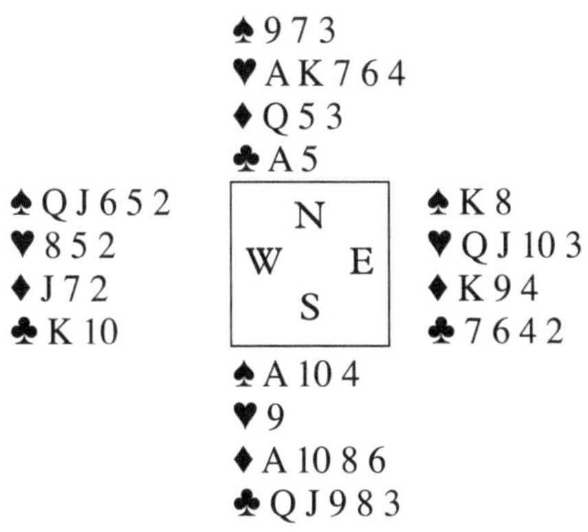

West	**North**	**East**	**South**
1 ♠	Pass	I NT	Pass
Pass	Dble	Pass	Pass
2 ♣	Pass	Pass	Dble
2 ♦	Pass	Pass	Dble
Redble	Pass	2 ♥	Pass
Pass	Dble	Pass	Pass
2 ♠	Pass	Pass	2 NT
Pass	3 ♥	Dble	3 NT
Pass	Pass	Dble	Pass
Pass	Redble	Pass	4 ♣
Pass	4 ♥	Dble	Pass
Pass	5 ♣	Pass	Pass
Dble	Pass	Pass	Redble
Pass	Pass	Pass	

West's psychic bids and East's psychic doubles managed to confuse North–South into bidding to the wrong contract. Three No-trumps was probably a safer option, although, as it happened, Five Clubs (redoubled) made for a better score.

West led ♠5 and South ducked the first round, won by East's king. Declarer won the spade return with the ace and then set about trumps. West covered ♣Q with the king, so declarer took his ace and returned to hand with ♣J. Two more rounds took care of trumps.

Declarer led ♦10 to West's jack, dummy's queen and East's king. East led ♥Q (whereas a spade would put the contract down), won by dummy's king. South's last spade was discarded on dummy's ♥A, and dummy's ♦5 was covered by ♦8 in hand, thus finessing the nine. Two more diamond tricks followed, making Five Clubs (redoubled). Forty minutes after the deal.

Many years later, in *Bridge Magazine* (January 1996), Peter Hawkes of Wallingford, Oxfordshire, suggested a competition for the longest credible bidding sequence. 'All bids must be plausible (even if not well judged), sufficient, not too repetitive, and consistent with a 52-card lay-out to be provided by the entrant,' he said, having constructed an example with 79 bids. 'Only natural bids and commonly used conventions and treatments are allowed.'

In real life, a number of things would encourage the participants to move on more quickly. I am reminded of an evening of rubber bridge which stretched past midnight. One of the four finally said, 'I must go home after this hand.' We dealt the hand and then entered a long sequence of bidding which eventually sent the tired visitor into a trance.

'It's your call,' one of us said.

'I'm sorry,' he said, shaking himself awake. 'It's long past my bidtime.'

BLINDFOLD BRIDGE

ENGLAND, JANUARY 1939

North–South are having a successful evening. The high cards are falling their way and they are cashing in. They are 'in the zone', as sportsmen say. North deals and bids immediately, without looking at his cards.

'One No-trump,' he says, laughing.

'Two No-trumps,' says South, whose hand is also face-down on the table.

'Three No-trumps,' says North, laughing even harder.

'Come on, play properly,' says a disgruntled East.

North reluctantly picks up his hand. 'One No-trump,' he says, stretching his values a little and laughing even harder.

'Pass.'

'Two No-trumps,' says South, even though it is not quite the correct textbook bid.

'Pass.'

'Three No-trumps,' says North, clutching his stomach. He is laughing so hard that he has not noticed that East and West are collecting their coats to go home.

'I think we'd have made it, too,' says South a few minutes later, when they are alone.

The above example may be some people's idea of 'blindfold bridge', but it was not the way the game was played in front of the television cameras in January 1939.

As G C H Fox wrote in his series 'A Brief History of Bridge' (*Bridge Magazine*, November 1994):

> Blindfold bridge is played without cards and entirely from memory. The players were given their cards for thirty seconds. The cards were then taken away and blank cards substituted. The bidding proceeded in the normal way, and when dummy was put down the real cards were laid out. In the play the exact cards were called out.

Players were penalised ten points when they erred in remembering the cards correctly. Here is an example:

Dealer South. Game All.

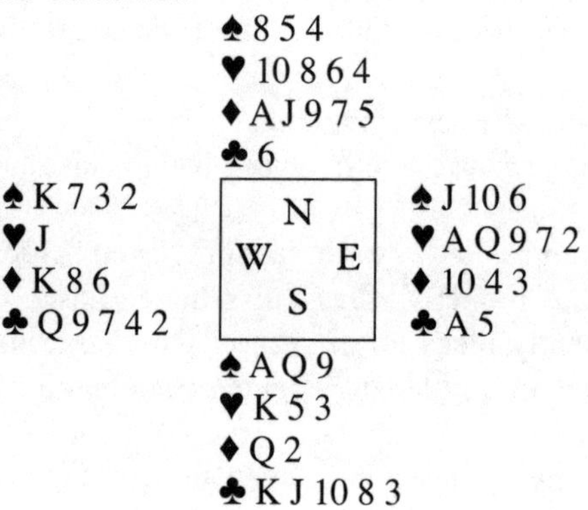

West	**North**	**East**	**South**
			1 ♣
Pass	1 ♦	1♥	1 NT
All Pass			

West led ♥J and the four was played from the table. East could not remember the denomination of his fifth heart. He called for the three instead of the two. The referee immediately awarded ten points to North–South. Judging by the layout of the cards, North–South took those points hungrily.

If you wish to try blindfold bridge at the kitchen table, I suggest that dummy acts as referee, moving around the table to check that the card-calling is correct. I shall leave it to you to decide whether to trust each other to keep eyes closed or use real blindfolds. You will need to trust your opponents as well as your partner.

Blindfold bridge may be a useful training aid for memory and concentration. It may also help players to discover a better awareness of the whole hand. Indeed, it is not dissimilar to the game played by blind people, who use special Braille packs of cards and rely on other players calling out the contents of dummy and each card played. Such special packs can be obtained through the Royal National Institute for the Blind.

ENGLAND UPSET BY WALES

THE CAMROSE CUP, 1939

The Camrose Trophy competition was introduced in 1937. Five countries – Eire, England, Northern Ireland, Scotland and Wales – played a series of two-day international matches against each other. England won all four of their matches in 1937 and again in 1938, but their first match in 1939, against Wales, produced a real upset. A large swing on one hand was enough to decide the 100-board match.

Dealer South. Game All.

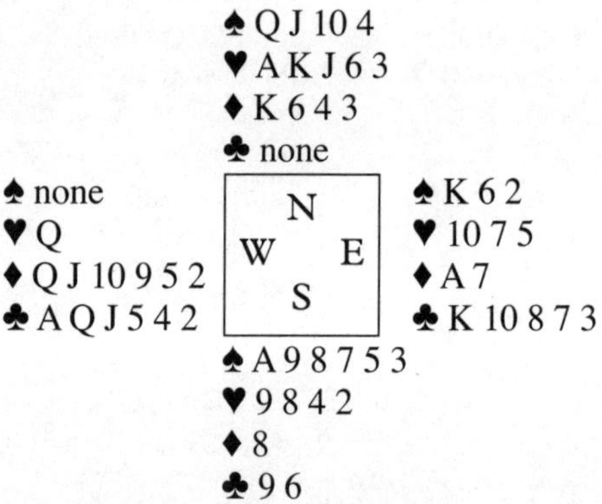

North: ♠ Q J 10 4 ♥ A K J 6 3 ♦ K 6 4 3 ♣ none

West: ♠ none ♥ Q ♦ Q J 10 9 5 2 ♣ A Q J 5 4 2

East: ♠ K 6 2 ♥ 10 7 5 ♦ A 7 ♣ K 10 8 7 3

South: ♠ A 9 8 7 5 3 ♥ 9 8 4 2 ♦ 8 ♣ 9 6

Room 1

West	**North**	**East**	**South**
England	*Wales*	*England*	*Wales*
			Pass
1 ♦	1 ♥	2 ♣	2 ♠
3 ♠	4 ♠	Pass	Pass
5 ♣	5 ♠	Dble	Pass
6 ♣	6 ♠	Dble	All Pass

Simon Rivlin, sitting North, correctly realised that a sacrifice was called for. He pressed on to Six Spades. Some sacrifice! West led ♣A and declarer made twelve tricks for 1,610 points.

In the other room, with England North–South, the outcome was very different.

Room 2

West	**North**	**East**	**South**
Wales	*England*	*Wales*	*England*
			Pass
1 ♦	1 ♥	Dble	Pass
2 ♣	Pass	3 ♣	3 ♥
4 ♣	4 ♥	5 ♣	All Pass

West might have thought that a slam was possible, but his pass stopped a sacrifice in hearts. North led ♠Q and declarer made all thirteen tricks for 640 points.

The swing on the hand was 2,250 points and England lost the match by 1,610 points. Despite the defeat by Wales, they won the Camrose Cup in 1939 and retained the trophy until Scotland won in 1964.

CARDS FOR EVERY OCCASION

LONDON, JUNE 1939

My first and only attempt to play bridge on an upper-floor balcony ended halfway through the first trick. A light breeze arrived unannounced and three cards from dummy flew off towards the railings. Two players chased the flying cards and the others held down the remaining cards in dummy.

'I think we should go inside,' said one player.

We all agreed.

I was badly prepared for that occasion. I now know better, because I have read Angela's column in *Bridge Magazine* (June 1939):

> Failing a garden, a flat roof on the top of a block of London flats is the next best thing for a game of bridge in the sunshine. I have recently been spending several warm weekends, playing outdoor bridge in the middle of the West End. So much so that a friend asked me if I had got my tan in the south of France, and when I replied: 'No, in Marylebone High Street,' she thought I was being funny.
>
> Now the one absolute essential for a game of this sort is a pack – or better still two packs – of aluminium cards. These are heavy enough to sit still on the table and not flutter away at the first puff of wind, yet they are quite thin and very easy to handle. I have had mine for several years now, and they are quite as good as new. I believe I paid 8/6 [43p] for them, which I thought quite a lot at the time, but they have been 'cheap at the price'.

I wish I had found a pack of aluminium cards some years ago – for playing not only in gardens and on balconies, but in some of the draughty places I have lived in. Or, alternatively, it would help to find a creative partner. The right inventor may be able to knock up aluminium cards, waterproof packs (for use on boats), leather cards (like those used by 16th-century Spanish soldiers), 65-card packs, 60-card packs, wide cards, narrow cards, photographic cards, automatic shuffling machines and various stacking devices for those whose fingers cannot hold cards.

Recently, we have seen packs with suits coloured red, blue, green and black rather than red and black. French cards have confused some tournament players with their different lettering – R for *roi* and V for *valet* – but the organisers of France's Omnium competition, first played in 1963, introduced cards with coded perforated edges so that each player could identify which thirteen cards were theirs.

Cards for every occasion.

BRIDGE ROLLS AND OTHER STRANGE HANDFULS

ON THE TROLLEY OR AT THE TABLE, 1939

I enjoy columns written by experts, but they rarely deal with the real challenges faced by players at bridge clubs:

> Who buys the tea and coffee?
> How do we ensure the milk is fresh?
> Should we hire someone to do the washing-up?
> How do we stop the Girl Guides from taking our biscuits?

Many writers have contributed to the 'cook and deal' genre, including Della Lutes (*Bridge Food for Bridge Fans*), Molly Anderson (*Bridge Party Hostess*), Nicola Cox (*The Bridge Players' Supper Book*) and Angela and Simon Ainger (*Simple Menus and Movements for Social Bridge*). The emphasis is on pre-prepared dishes which need only a finishing touch from the next dummy.

Some hosts prefer gourmet bridge evenings that leave time for only two or three hands, with guests dressing for dinner. The more professional bridge players equip themselves with the bare essentials – say, a bucket of peanuts and enough crisps to last a dozen rubbers.

In 1954, Gordon Hammond dealt with food and drink as part of a series of *Contract Bridge Journal* articles on duplicate-bridge evenings in the home:

> Finally, comes the question of refreshment. The essential thing is to be host or hostess for the first event, when, with the novelty of

inauguration, tea and buns are quite adequate. As each of the invitees will feel constrained to arrange subsequent matches, the scale of refreshment will become more and more elaborate as each host and hostess seeks to outshine his or her predecessor. With any luck, the final event of the series will be accompanied by champagne and a seven-course dinner, which will show a pretty good return on your original investment of tea and buns.

Angela of *Bridge Magazine* often referred to the bridge roll, a small soft bread roll which safely holds its filling. I have always assumed that bridge rolls were developed for bridge parties in the 1920s and 1930s, but have found no reference to their origin, not even in Elizabeth David's definitive *English Bread and Yeast Cooking*. Among Angela's suggested bridge-roll fillings was this one from June 1939:

> Split and butter them on both sides (don't be stingy) then lay a nice bit of white lettuce leaf as a foundation. Next make a mixture of 'gentleman's relish' (about a quarter of the pot); this will keep quite well in a really cool place), a hard-boiled egg, which has been finely minced, white and yolk, and soften the relish and egg with a little mayonnaise, either home-made or of the bottle variety. By the way, don't get the consistency too soppy [*sic*], and add just a mere suspicion of French mustard (this item is not essential).

Angela duly came up with another the next month:

> The foundation is the same, of course: i.e., your small bridge rolls, split and well buttered, on which you lay very thin slices of beetroot, sprinkled with the merest soupçon of vinegar. Then you proceed to make a sort of purée of any kind of cream cheese you fancy (pommel or St Ivel or Petit Suisse) which you mix with very finely chopped orange (about half an orange to twelve rolls). This you spread on to the beetroot foundation, and you will be surprised how well the different flavourings shake down together.

BRIDGE IN BATTLE

AROUND THE WORLD, 1940–5

One time in Italy, a bridge game was threatened by a nearby battle.

'Two Diamonds,' said the next bidder, as a shell exploded.

His partner misheard the bid as 'Three Diamonds'. Since Two Diamonds was enough for game, Three Diamonds must have been an invitation to explore slam possibilities.

'Six Diamonds,' said the partner.

The hand went down and the noise of military action continued. The last four tricks were made with the players lying on their stomachs.

During the Second World War, bridge appeared in plenty of unusual locations. In Britain, people sometimes stayed in air-raid shelters to complete a rubber after the 'all-clear' had been sounded, and the Lederer Bridge Club in Hyde Park Place, London, was destroyed by a bomb in 1941. In the Middle East one RAF serviceman wrote home with elaborate stories of playing bridge in an environment of sun, sand and flies. 'I hope you will not get the impression that we do nothing but play bridge,' he said in his letter. 'No, we sometimes play solo.'

One place strong on wartime bridge was Gibraltar, the disputed territory to the south of Spain. Britain was granted sovereignty of Gibraltar under the Treaty of Utrecht (1713), but the Spanish claim resulted in a long-standing economic blockade. During the Second World War there was a period when Gibraltar was the only United Nations foothold on the continent of Europe. Bridge was often played in spartan conditions.

One of Gibraltar's most famous bridge games was that played by General Dwight Eisenhower, General Mark Clark, General A M Gruenther and Commander Harry Butcher in November 1942. The game took place while they waited for news of the Casablanca landings. One can almost visualise Humphrey Bogart saying to Ingrid Bergman, 'Here's looking at your hand, kid.'

When civilians returned to Gibraltar, bridge continued to form an integral part of their lives. Here is a hand from that time, two servicemen against two civilians.

Dealer East. East–West Game.

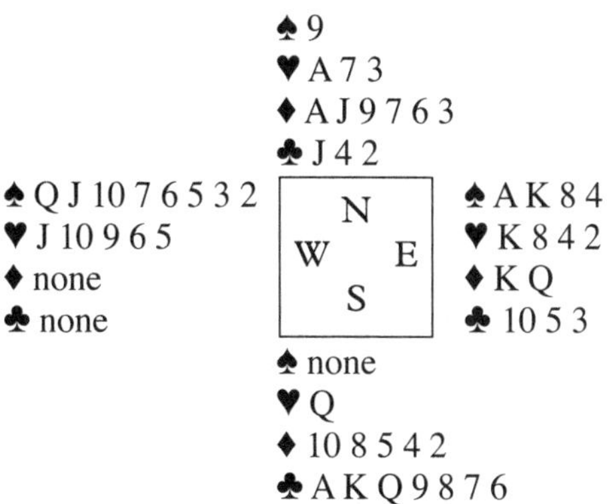

West	North	East	South
		1 ♠	5 ♣
5 ♠	6 ♣	Dble	Pass
6 ♠	Dble	Pass	7 ♣
Pass	Pass	Dble	All Pass

West led ♥J and the contract went one off for a deficit of 100 points. This may have been a good sacrifice, as Six Spades makes if West guesses the hearts correctly.

PRISONER-OF-WAR CAMPS

EUROPE AND THE FAR EAST, 1940–5

In an article for *Contract Bridge Journal* (September 1947), Mr J G Gordon explained how bridge had helped prisoners of war retain mental balance during their captivity. 'No other game could have assisted us so well,' he said.

When Gordon was taken prisoner, in 1940, it was hard to play bridge in the camps. Cards had to be improvised and prisoners had to learn the game's basics. Three years later, the Red Cross was delivering cards and bridge books, and special rooms were set aside for bridge. Pairs competitions took place once a month and teams of four played regularly. In 1944 a series of exhibition matches was organised at one camp and spectators were able to follow play in the open room as messengers hung large cards on a specially designed board.

'Take a walk around with me,' wrote Gordon, recreating the scene.

> See that Colonel there? Couldn't play at all three years ago; watch him now with fierce intensity planning a pseudo-squeeze. The Major playing against him got in a nice inferential force last hand, but even that didn't atone in the eyes of his partner (a Brigadier) for misinterpreting the Brig's forcing pass earlier in the afternoon. In a word, bridge has become the principal means of keeping occupied the minds of half the camp, occupied against the ever-present menace of boredom which, behind the wire, is the forerunner of mental instability.

Life in PoW camps was not always as civilised as Gordon's account sounds. A young South African, Derrick Hirsch, was described as 'the driving force behind the amazing bridge organisation in one of the most festering camps in Siam' and the Japanese did not always approve. One knocked out four of Hirsch's teeth with the butt of a rifle as punishment for playing bridge. Another time Hirsch was forced to stand to attention outside the guard room for 48 consecutive hours.

In Hirsch's camp, the culmination of the bridge season was an 'international' match between the Dutch PoWs and the British PoWs (who included South Africans and Americans). This deal arose in the normal way from a perfectly shuffled pack. Even the Japanese guards found it interesting.

Dealer North. Game All.

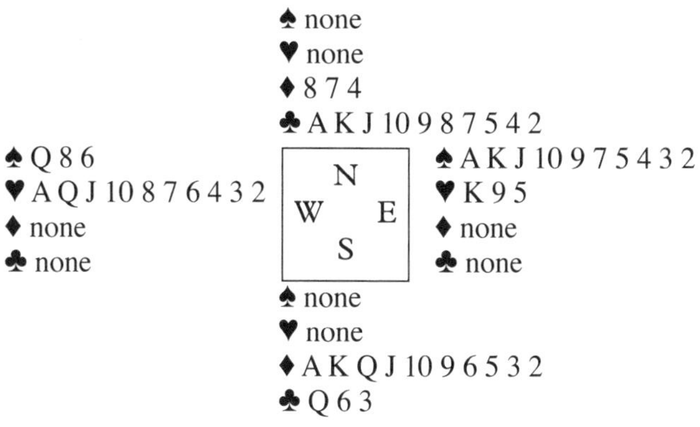

Room 1

West	**North**	**East**	**South**
Britain	*Holland*	*Britain*	*Holland*
	5 ♣	5 ♠	7 ♦
7 ♥	All Pass		

Room 2

West	**North**	**East**	**South**
Holland	*Britain*	*Holland*	*Britain*
	1 ♣	Dble	2 ♦
4 ♥	4 ♠	7 ♠	7 NT
Dble	All Pass		

In Room 1 the bidding was quickly over. And so was the play, when West's lay-down claimed the contract to score 2,210 points for Britain.

In Room 2, there was a more unusual development. The British North–South were playing what they thought was the Stern Austrian system, which may help explain the bids of One Club and Two Diamonds. North wanted to play the hand in clubs but also wanted to make an asking bid in diamonds. He settled for Four Spades as a waiting bid. The Dutch East didn't believe North and shot to Seven Spades.

Then it came to South. He assumed that North did not have a real club suit as he had not repeated them. South therefore deduced that his partner's Austrian-system One Club meant he had at least three spades and something in hearts – either ♥A or ♥K and ♥Q. Even better, if East has ten spades and North has three, then West will have a void in that suit and cannot lead it. Hence Seven No-trumps may be only one or two down, and Seven Spades might make.

Oh dear.

As soon as South saw dummy, he must have realised that it was impossible for him to get the lead. Thirteen down. I think that meant 3,800 points to the Dutch.

North–South had the minors and East–West had the majors. And, who knows, they may even have had a major playing for them.

EVERYBODY INTERESTED

LYMINGTON, HAMPSHIRE, 1947

This teasing rubber deal, submitted to *Contract Bridge Journal* by Colonel A Williams-Freeman, kept everybody interested.

Dealer South. East–West Game.

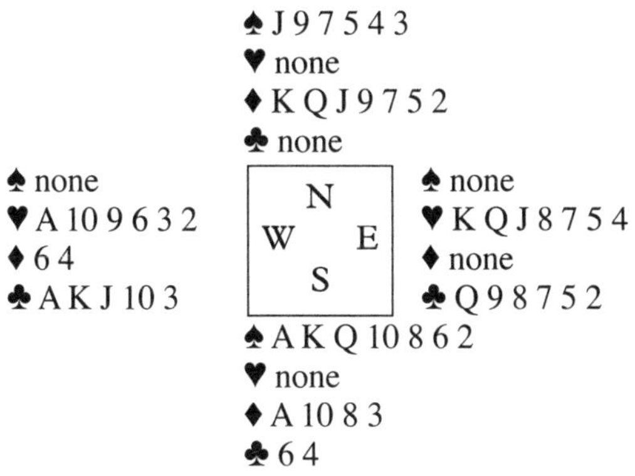

West	North	East	South
			4 ♠
5 ♥	6 ♠	7 ♥ (i)	7 ♠
Dble	Redble	All Pass	

(i) West's first bid was actually an insufficient Six Hearts

The trumps split zero–zero and Seven Spades was a lay-down. Seven Hearts would have been too.

THE RASPBERRY JAM CONUNDRUM

BIRMINGHAM, MAY 1947

The Hubert Phillips Bowl semi-final between the Jacobs team (Birmingham) and the Frith team (Nottingham) was closely contested. It was decided by one particular board, the outcome of which was debated for months afterwards. The saga became known as the Raspberry Jam Conundrum.

When Major Mannion, representing the Frith team, picked up his thirteen cards, the hand had already been played in the other room. Major Mannion's right-hand opponent opened One Spade and the Major overcalled Two Hearts. The contract was doubled and Major Mannion was vulnerable.

The Major's left-hand opponent respected his partner's opening bid and led a spade, which Major Mannion trumped. He later ruffed two further rounds of spades. Unfortunately, towards the end of the hand it transpired that Major Mannion was one card short. The contract looked to be two down (as far as anyone can tell in these situations).

Everyone searched high and low for the missing card. Those aware of the history of missing cards know where to look – on the floor, in shoes, under coffee cups, in trouser turn-ups, under chair cushions and up sleeves. In this case none of these applied. Eventually the missing card was found stuck firmly to the small heart used by declarer to trump the first round of spades. Naturally the missing card was a spade.

Defence claimed that Major Mannion appeared to be technically liable for three revokes. Eventually the rival captains agreed that the revoke claim was valid and four tricks were transferred to the defending side. Declarer was thus six down, for a penalty of 1,700 points, enough to decide the match. Major Mannion's team had held a good lead before this hand, but the Jacobs team now went on to win by a slender margin (and later won the final at the Cheltenham Congress).

Things soon became very sticky, as summarised by *Contract Bridge Journal* (November 1947):

> Piquancy was added to the discussion that followed by the allegation that the two cards in question were stuck together through the liberal misuse of jam by Mannion's *vis-à-vis* in Room 1, where the board had been played round about the time that a dish of jam pastries had been handed round the room, although this suggestion was hotly denied by the home players.

When the matter was referred to the committee of the Portland Club, the committee reiterated the point that these cases should be determined by the players (or director) following the fairest procedure in view of the facts of the particular case. But there was an added twist to the saga, as spelled out by the Portland Club: 'The committee further decided that no revoke took place, the only spade in South's hand having been played to the first spade trick, however peculiar the manner in which it was played.'

The moral of the story is apparent: raspberry jam pastries should be served carefully at bridge tables.

EVERYBODY OFF

LONDON, 1947

Misfits are not normally as classic as Angela's example on page 60, but their effect can be just as powerful. This hand could have been dealt by a sadist. In the final of the *Daily Telegraph* competition, ten out of ten North–South pairs went down.

Dealer North. Game All.

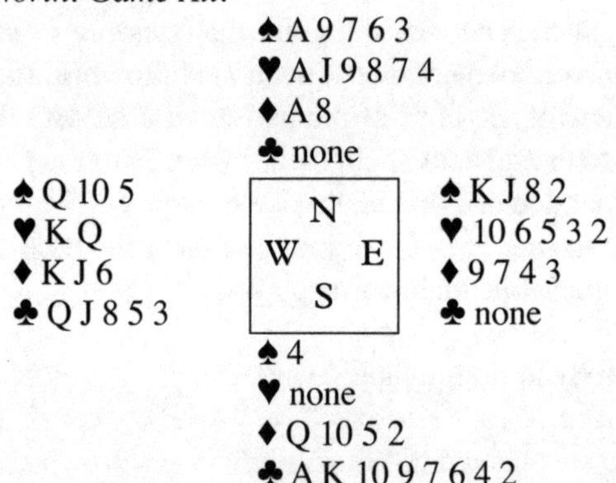

West	**North**	**East**	**South**
	1 ♥	Dble	2 ♣
Dble	2 ♠	Dble	3 ♣
Dble	3 ♠	Dble	4 ♣
Dble	4 ♥	Dble	5 ♣
Dble	6 ♣	Pass	Pass
Dble	All Pass		

At all except one table, South played the contract in clubs (see summary below), but Three No-trumps was off as well.

Contract	Tricks	Minus
6 ♣ (Dble)	9	800
6 ♣ (Dble)	10	500
6 ♣	10	200
5 ♣	10	100
5 ♣ (Dble)	10	200
5 ♣ (Dble)	9	500
5 ♣	9	200
4 ♣ (Dble)	9	200
4 ♣ (Dble)	9	200
3 NT (Dble)	8	200

The most comical bidding sequence is the one shown. How many calling sequences have seen nine doubles?

It took very careful play to make ten tricks in clubs. At one table West led ♥K, which declarer took with dummy's ace while discarding a diamond from hand. A heart ruff was followed by ♣K and then bad news.

'No clubs?' queried South.

'No,' said East. 'No clubs.'

'Look again and see if you can find one – even a little one.'

'Sorry, not one,' confirmed East.

He did not look sorry.

Declarer ran ♠4 to dummy's ace, ruffed a small spade, and then ♣9 lost to the jack. West's return of a low spade was ruffed.

A low trump was played to West's eight. West now had to lead a trump or a diamond to give North the tenth trick.

Overall, the ten hands cost ten North–South partnerships 3,100 points. And these were very good players.

21 TRICKS IN SPADES

HOLLAND VS. FRANCE, 1948

In *The Bridge Immortals* (1967), Victor Mollo describes this hand as 'an unusual situation'. The Dutch international Cornelius 'Bob' Slavenburg helped his team make 21 tricks with spades as trumps. The Dutch East–West pair bid Six Spades in one room and made thirteen tricks, and their North–South pair in the other room bid and made Two Spades.

Dealer East.

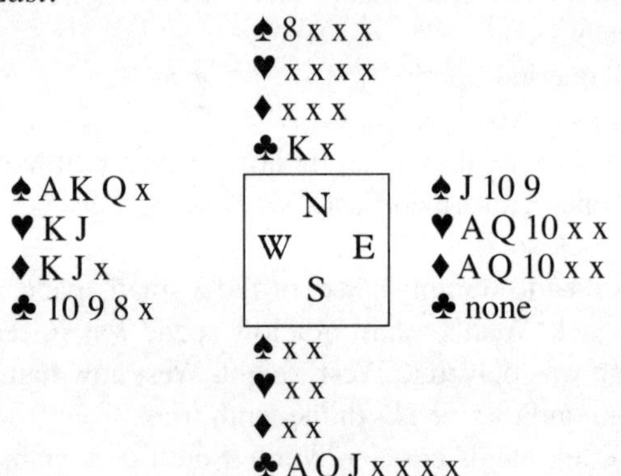

West	North	East	South
			Slavenburg
		1 ♥	1 ♠(i)
Dble	Pass	Pass	2 ♣
Dble	2 ♠ (ii)	All Pass (iii)	

(i) A psychic
(ii) My spades are better than my clubs, partner
(iii) Slavenburg reckoned that if he bid Three Clubs, his partner would bid Three Spades, so he settled for the penalty

The Dutch were disappointed with their contract of Six Spades in Room 1. They recognised that a grand slam was available in spades, hearts or diamonds, and they expected the French to find a better contract in Room 2. Instead Bob Slavenburg came up with his amazing contract.

Defending Two Spades, West decided to stop all ruffing potential. He led ♠A and followed up with ♠K and ♠Q. He was surprised to see his partner play the nine and ten, then astonished when ♠J appeared. West led a club next – it looked safer than the red suits.

Slavenburg won the trick with dummy's ♣K. He drew the last trump with dummy's eight and then cashed six more club tricks.

Six Spades plus one in Room 1. Two Spades made in Room 2. All points to Holland.

A STRAIGHTFORWARD DEAL

BLACKPOOL, SEPTEMBER 1948

This hand was played in a duplicate pairs competition at Blackpool Bridge Club. How would you open as South?

Dealer South.

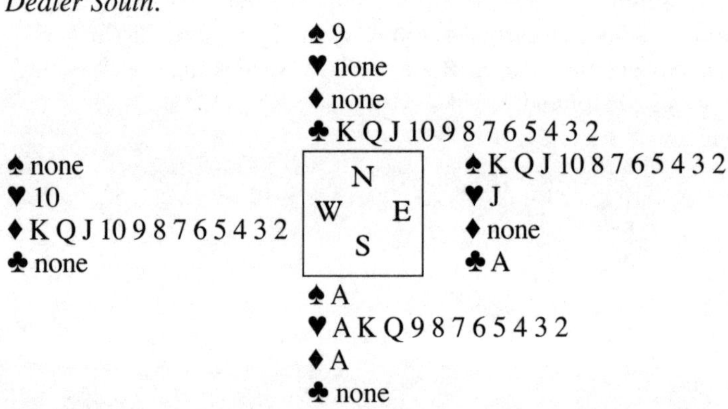

Every South at the club opened Seven Hearts. Most opponents sacrificed in Seven Spades, which was always doubled and always two down. Two Souths played in Seven Hearts and one in Seven Hearts (redoubled), but they were all two off. West led a diamond for East to ruff and East returned a spade for a ruff. (South's 'best' opening bid is Seven No-trumps.)

The honorary secretary of the Blackpool club assured the public that this wasn't a goulash night – it was 'a straightforward deal'.

TOO GOOD TO BE TRUE

ENGLAND, 1948

This deal arose on a duplicate night at a club in England. What would you bid if you were South?

Dealer South.

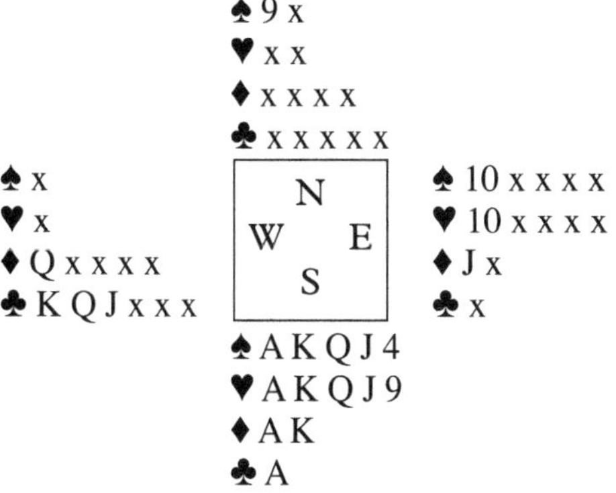

This time every South in the club except one opened Seven No-trumps. One quick-thinking pessimist bid Six No-trumps, thinking the 31-point hand was too good to be true. In fact, it needed an end-play to make Six No-trumps.

Lucky in points, unlucky in partner's points. Lucky in points, unlucky in play.

A HEARTBREAKER

ENGLAND, 1948

According to *The Bridge Players' Encyclopedia*, a heartbreaker is 'a term applied to a hand that fails to live up to one's original expectation of it'. The term is most commonly applied to a defensive hand that initially looks capable of chalking up plenty of penalty points.

Maybe bridge experts have less experience of heartbreakers than the amateur. Until it comes to freaks. A freak hand can occasionally convert a very experienced player into a broken-hearted, tearful wreck. Here is an example. The hand was recalled by the bridge correspondent of *The Times* ten years after it had occurred. The players were all top-class internationals and one of them ended the hand in tears.

Dealer North. North–South Game.

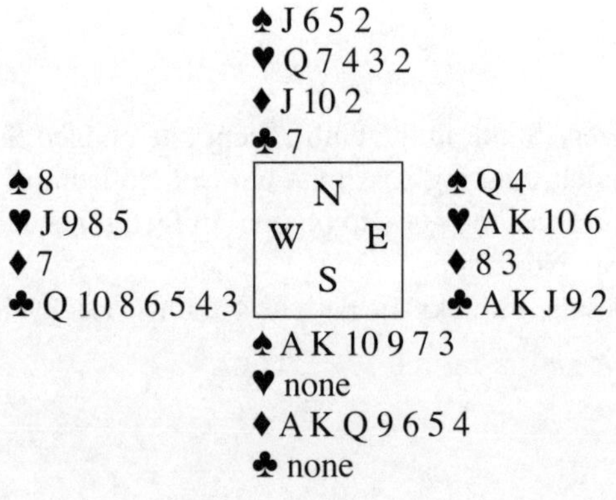

West	**North**	**East**	**South**
	Pass	1 ♣	2 ♠
4 ♣	4 ♠	6 ♣	6 ♠
Pass	Pass	Dble	Pass
Pass	Redble	All Pass	

North's redouble was an attempt to drive opponents into Seven Clubs. East–West would have none of it – East was sure of setting the small slam. But East held a heartbreaker and West had a triangle (three points).

In fact Seven Spades makes on any lead. East's seventeen points might as well have counted as zero. West's hand was not worth anything either.

A solid grand slam off twenty high-card points. No wonder one of the players cried at the end. No prizes for guessing which one.

SLAM ON A YARBOROUGH

LONDON, 1949

This hand was dealt in a rubber game at a London club. North–South thought they were sacrificing in Six Clubs but in fact the contract made. This was astonishing as North had only seven points and South (declarer) had a yarborough (no card higher than a nine).

The odds of holding a yarborough are 1,827 to one. The odds of making a slam with one are somewhat longer. A yarborough is known by many other names, such as 'a load of rubbish', 'a hand like a foot' and 'train tickets'. I have seen players bark, 'Who dealt?' as if they were looking for someone to blame. But this hand proves that points are not everything.

Dealer West. East–West Game.

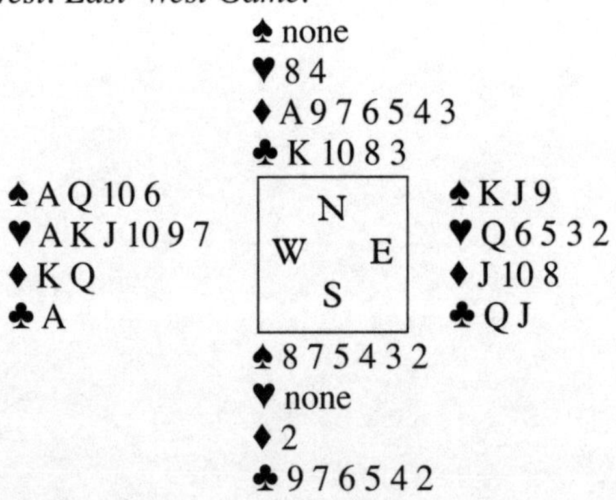

West	**North**	**East**	**South**
2 ♣	2 ♦	2 NT	3 ♠
Dble	4 ♦	Dble	5 ♣
5 ♥	6 ♣	Pass	Pass
Dble	All Pass		

West led ♥K. Declarer ruffed in hand and led a small club. When West played the singleton ace, declarer played low from dummy.

One trick each.

West's return of ♦K lost to declarer's ace. Then declarer's ♣K took care of East's queen.

Diamond ruff. Spade ruff. Diamond ruff. Spade ruff.

Three established diamonds in dummy. And the last two trumps.

A small slam on a yarborough with 33 missing points. Doubled too.

Do you think the East–West partnership regretted not bidding Six Hearts?

DOWN TO THE LAST HAND (TWICE)

PARIS, FRANCE, 1949

The 1949 Women's European Championships was one of the most exciting contests ever played. It ended with a hand that was described by one magazine as the stuff of a novel or film. It was 'good theatre, but highly improbable'.

Denmark retained their European title by beating Sweden on the last board of the final league match. With one board to play, Denmark trailed Sweden by one match point and needed to gain five match points on the hand in order to pip France and win the overall competition. In the Closed Room, Sweden bid Four Hearts and made eleven tricks. Experts agreed that there was no more to be taken from the hand and no possibility of a slam. Only a miracle could help Denmark win the tournament, but a miracle duly arrived.

When the board arrived in the Open Room, the players picked out their cards and prepared for the bidding. Only then did one of the Swedish players realise that she had fourteen cards. Another player had twelve. They had all looked at their cards, so the tournament director ordered a fresh deal.

The Championships now depended on this redealt hand, with Denmark still needing a swing of five match points to beat France. The contract was Three No-trumps in both rooms. Denmark made their Three No-trumps but Sweden went one down in theirs. The resulting two Victory Points enabled Denmark to tie with France on points. In the event of a tie, the outcome was decided by the result of the league match between the two countries. As Denmark had beaten France in their match, they won the Championships.

There are other examples of hands being redealt in tournaments – when the cards are played the same way in both rooms, or when a board has been inadvertently rotated – but this is a rare example of it happening on the last hand in such a close finish. It is probably not the closest finish ever, though. A few months earlier, at the 1948 Open Pairs at the North American Winter National Tournament, Helen Sobel and Margaret Wagar won by 955.2223 match points to the 955.2179 scored by Peter Levintritt and Edson Wood. The victory margin of .0044 match points resulted from the complicated system used to factor down the point carry-overs from one round to the next. That is one of the great intellectual beauties of bridge – understanding the scoring system can be as demanding as playing the hands.

DISTURBING THE PEACE

ENGLAND, 1949

This hand gains quirkiness in the context of the relationships between the players. Hands may be inherently strange, but the play can become strange in order to satisfy some raw emotion, such as revenge, pride or the need to humiliate. Here, South saw a once-in-a-lifetime opportunity to disturb West's serenity.

Dealer North. Love All.

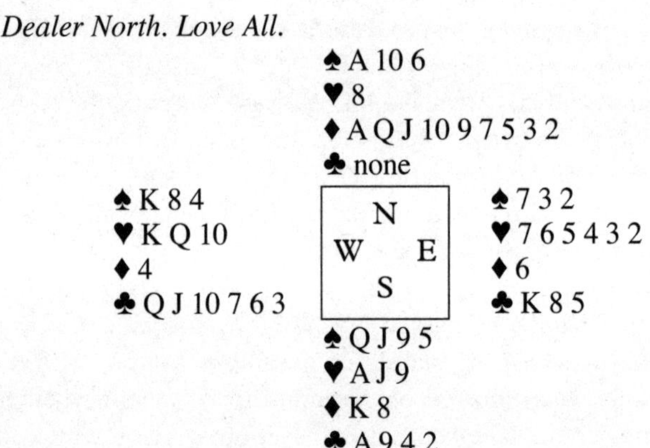

West	North	East	South
	1 ♦	Pass	3 NT
Pass	4 NT	Pass	5 ♥
Pass	7 NT	Pass	Pass
Dble	Redble	All Pass	

After North had used Blackwood to check on the missing two aces, South found himself in Seven No-trumps (redoubled). West's opening lead was ♣Q, signalling top of a run. East went up with her ♣K to show West where the king was and indicate that West's ♣J was a master.

Sitting West was a woman of impeccable calm. In all her years at the club she had never lost her temper, never shown any emotion. For some reason South decided his role in life was to be the one to ruffle her long-standing serenity. Some people are like that.

South weighed up the options. He assumed from West's double that West had the two outstanding kings. Rather than take the spade finesse, he decided to see how much tension he could introduce to West's wonderfully phlegmatic nature.

South slowly played through his winning diamonds. When dummy was reduced to ♠A, ♠10, ♥8, ♦3 and ♦2, declarer suspected that West held ♠K, ♠x, ♥K, ♥Q and ♣J. He led the last two diamonds, and West had to find two painful discards. South succeeded in disrupting West's calm demeanour.

This subtle example of manipulation and cruelty can be filed alongside lapses such as 'the emotional double' (usually followed by the rational redouble) or 'the double in a rage' (often followed by partner in a rage). There are more flagrant examples of raw emotion – smoking guns, marital breakdown, shouting matches, smashed tables, flying cards, angry partners playing back to back and walk-outs which upset the table arrangements.

One legendary tale concerns a pair who split up without playing a card. The first hand was passed out and they got into a raging argument about who was to blame for missing a contract of Two No-trumps. This was followed by a second row – about whether Two No-trumps could have been made. 'I'm not playing with you any more,' said one, storming out.

WHEN DEFENCE CLAIMED 150 HONOURS

LONDON, 1949

I suspect there was emotion wrapped up in the following bidding sequence. Both pairs rejected obvious opportunities in favour of an unlikely contract and likely conflict. North–South played Two Diamonds (redoubled) on a three–zero split and made the contract.

Dealer East. Game All.

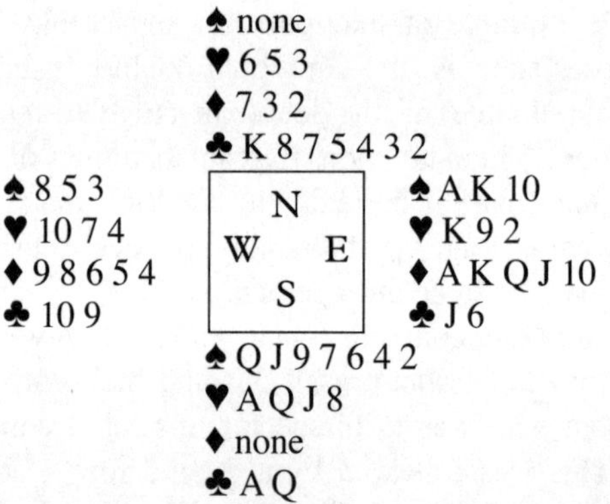

♠ none
♥ 6 5 3
♦ 7 3 2
♣ K 8 7 5 4 3 2

♠ 8 5 3
♥ 10 7 4
♦ 9 8 6 5 4
♣ 10 9

♠ A K 10
♥ K 9 2
♦ A K Q J 10
♣ J 6

♠ Q J 9 7 6 4 2
♥ A Q J 8
♦ none
♣ A Q

West	North	East	South
		1 ♦	2 ♦
Dble	Pass	Pass	Redble
All Pass			

West led ♠8. South ruffed in dummy and led a small heart to the jack. When the finesse worked, declarer ruffed a spade and returned to ♥Q in hand. A third spade ruff used up the last of declarer's trumps with only ten other trumps still out. So much for trump control.

The hearts were evenly split, so declarer was able to return safely to ♥A. The first six tricks had now been won by declarer, who continued by cashing ♣A and ♣K before conceding the rest to defence's ten trumps.

'One-fifty for honours,' East said meekly, before asking his partner what was wrong with a trump lead.

Six Clubs would have been a better contract for North–South, but South may have enjoyed Two Diamonds more in the long run. It was a story to dine out on.

THREE NO-TRUMPS – EITHER WAY

LONDON, 1950

This curiosity was captured for posterity in *Bridge from The Times* (1950), a collection of columns from the London newspaper. When the hand was dealt for a pairs contest, there was a different outcome on each of the nine tables (see scoresheet below). The two most surprising results were at Table 2, where South made Three No-trumps (doubled), and Table 6, where West made Three No-trumps. It is an odd hand that makes Three No-trumps either way.

Plenty of leads could have put down these contracts, but such is real life.

Dealer North. East–West Game.

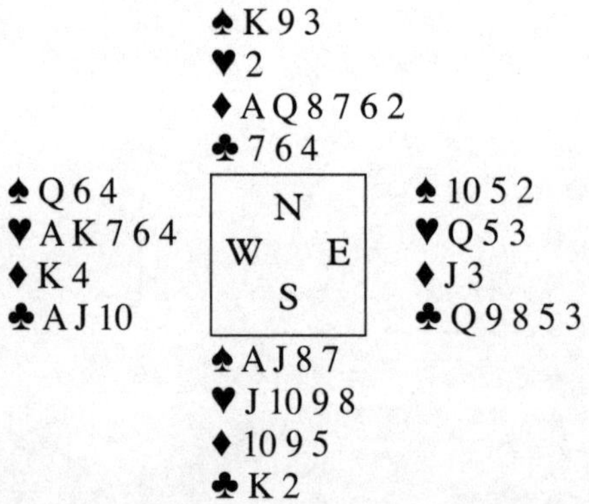

Table 2

West	**North**	**East**	**South**
	Pass	Pass	Pass
1 ♥	2 ♦	3 ♣	3 NT
Dble	All Pass		

Table 6

West	**North**	**East**	**South**
	Pass	Pass	Pass
1 NT	2 ♦	3 ♣	Pass
3 NT	All Pass		

At Table 2, West led ♣J to South's king. South led ♦10, which was covered by West's king and dummy's ace. Declarer then played ♦Q and the jack fell nicely. Declarer came back to hand with ♦2 to ♦5. Then he played ♠J. Again West covered, with the queen, and dummy's king won the trick.

Declarer cashed three diamond bosses from dummy while discarding three hearts from hand. East discarded ♠2 on a diamond, so East's ♠10 fell on South's ♠A, creating two more spade winners. Three No-trumps (doubled) made eleven tricks – six diamonds, four spades and ♣K.

At Table 6, where West was declarer in Three No-trumps, North led ♦7. Declarer won with dummy's jack and led ♣3 to his ten. He went back to dummy with ♥Q and led a second club, felling South's king. He overtook ♣J with dummy's queen and cashed two more club tricks. Two top hearts took his tally to nine tricks – three hearts, five clubs and ♦J.

Table 1	4 ♥	West	9	100	
Table 2	3 NT (Dble)	South	11	700	
Table 3	3 ♦ (Dble)	North	9	570	
Table 4	3 ♣	East	9		110
Table 5	3 ♦	North	9	110	
Table 6	3 NT	West	9		600
Table 7	3 ♥	West	9		140
Table 8	3 ♠ (Dble)	South	9	630	
Table 9	2 NT (Dble)	North	5		300

7,110 POINTS RESTING ON THE LEAD

USA, 1951

This is the tale of how one player learned that he should always lead his partner's suit against a One No-trump contract. The story first appeared in the *Barclay Bridge News*, and was later reproduced in the *Contract Bridge Journal* (October 1951).

At first the hands seem innocuous enough, but a simple seven-call bidding sequence turned it into something more dramatic.

Dealer East. Game All.

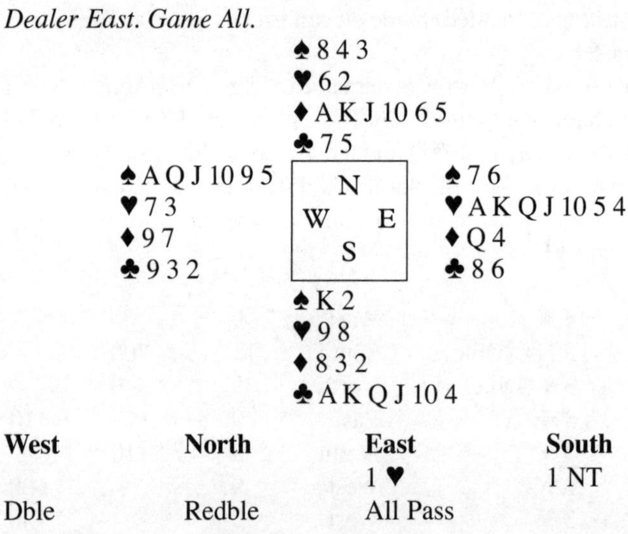

West	North	East	South
		1 ♥	1 NT
Dble	Redble	All Pass	

Please do not ask me to explain the bidding. The crucial aspect of the hand came when West contemplated his lead. Let us look inside his mind. Partner has bid One Heart but South must have a stop in hearts to bid One No-trump. I'll lead ♠Q.

Oh dear.

Declarer won ♠K on the first round and took all thirteen tricks for 3,110 points. West's partner was none too pleased. A heart lead would have netted East–West the first seven tricks, and East's spade return would have sealed all thirteen for defence (4,000 points the other way).

'The result, which proves nothing except that people are funny, caused turmoil, pandemonium, and an exchange of words that cannot be reprinted here or anywhere,' said the *Barclay Bridge News* correspondent. 'The declarer also has asked that his name be withheld so that he may remain at large.'

AN INTERNATIONAL PAR CONTEST

AUSTRALIA, 1951

In November 1951 the Australian Bridge Council staged an International Par Point Pairs Championship, thus reviving the idea of the World Bridge Olympics, held annually from 1932 to 1941. The hands were set by the 1950 Australasian Pairs champions, Michael Sullivan and H W Hiley.

Some people argue that Par Point Championships are the only true test of bridge skill. They take away the unpredictability of how opponents are playing. What is left is a need for precise bidding, correct player technique and logical deduction in order to gain maximum effect from the hand.

Here is the sample provided by the Australian Bridge Council in 1951. It was designed to attract entrants to the competition.

Dealer South.

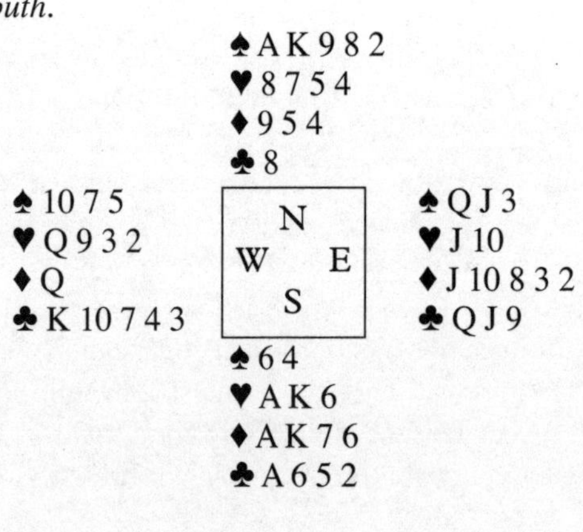

North–South scored four points for finishing the bidding in Three No-trumps or Four Spades. This was the official bidding:

West	**North**	**East**	**South**
			1 ♦
Pass	1 ♠	Pass	3 NT
All Pass			

In order to standardise the play a little, three of the players were given instruction slips on the hand.

South: take ♣A on third round and lead ♠4
East: continue clubs when in
West: play low on second round of clubs

Can you spot the point-winning play on this hand?

East–West were awarded eight points for defeating the contract, *but only if* West played ♠10 on the first round of spades.

Here was the official comment on the hand:

> When South, as directed, leads ♠4 at Trick 4, West should perceive that ducking in dummy will establish four tricks in the suit, which, added to South's five honours tricks, will be sufficient for game. West should scotch declarer's obvious intention by producing ♠10 when the four is led. This defence gives South a 'Hobson's Choice' of (a) ducking and permitting West to win two club tricks or (b) winning in dummy to surrender the long-card spade tricks and postpone defeat.

The Australian international par contest lasted until 1963. When a new par contest was introduced, in 1990, the organisers were able to take advantage of new technology. Personal computers displayed details of problems. As players typed in their suggested plays, the computers played for opponents, informed contestants of errors and time taken, and kept score. This new contest for Pamp Par Hands was described by Alan Truscott in the *New York Times* as 'the most difficult and challenging event in the history of bridge'.

SYMMETRY

ST PANCRAS TOWN HALL, LONDON, NOVEMBER 1951

This symmetrical hand occurred in a match at St Pancras Town Hall between St Pancras and Bethnal Green. The hand was passed out at both tables. The strangest thing was that such a hand was observed in its entirety and discovered. That was because it happened to occur in a match where the hands were recorded and redeals prohibited.

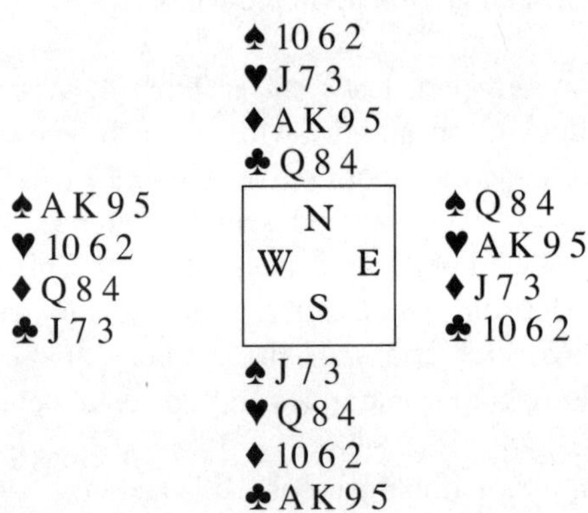

PASSING WITH OVER TWENTY POINTS – LESSON 1

ENGLAND, 1952

You are sitting North with a 25-point powerhouse. When is it acceptable to pass partner's opening bid?

Dealer South.

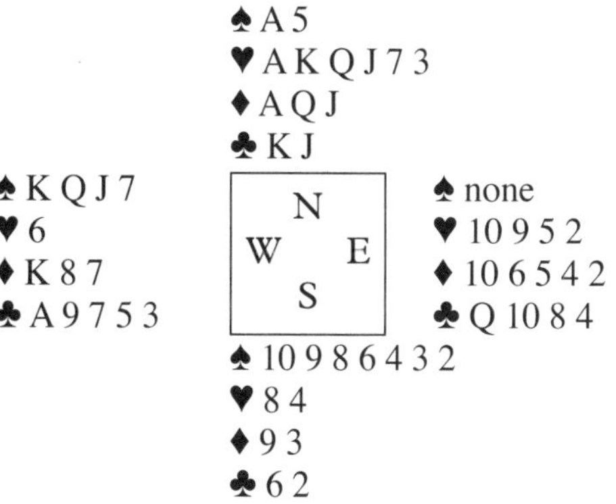

West	**North**	**East**	**South**
			3 ♠
Dble	All Pass		

Had North redoubled, East might have escaped into Four Clubs, which is one off. With no slam possible, Three Spades (doubled) was as good a game contract as any; it made nine tricks (but a small-club lead would have been interesting).

I bet South said, 'Thank you, partner.'

WORLD CHAMPIONS KNOCKED OUT IN FIRST ROUND

USA, 1953

This is the story of how four American world champions were eliminated from the first round of the Vanderbilt Cup, an annual American team-of-four contest which later became part of the Spring National Championships.

Jay Becker, John Crawford, Howard Schenken and Sam Stayman helped the USA to win the Bermuda Bowl World Championships in 1951 and 1953. All except Becker had also played in the 1950 winning American team. These stars, plus fifth team-member George Rapée, were favourites for the Vanderbilt Cup, but they were beaten in their first match by a team of unknowns. This unusual hand virtually decided matters.

Dealer North. Game All.

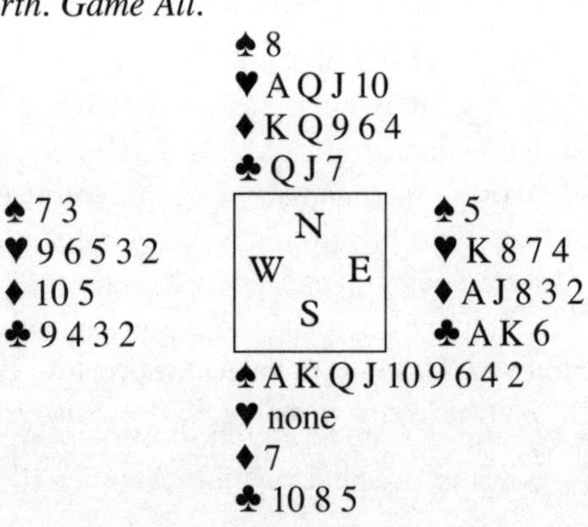

Room 1

West	**North**	**East**	**South**
Becker	*P. Atiyeh*	*Crawford*	*Malmame*
	1 ♥	2 ♦	3 ♠
Pass	3 NT	Pass	4 ♦
Pass	4 NT	Pass	6 ♠
Pass	Pass	Dble	All Pass

Room 2

West	**North**	**East**	**South**
F. Atiyeh	*Schenken*	*Perry*	*Stayman*
	1 ♥	2 ♦	4 NT
Pass	5 ♦	Pass	5 ♠
All Pass			

In Room 1, West led the only suit that could enable the slam to make. Assuming his partner's double was Lightner (requesting an unusual lead such as opponents' suit), West led ♥2. Declarer played the queen, ruffed the king and re-entered dummy with ♠8 in order to discard three clubs on three hearts. Declarer made twelve tricks for 1,660 points. (Had the world champions cashed their three winners, it would have been 500 points the other way – a swing of 2,160 points.)

In Room 2, South settled at Five Spades after a Blackwood enquiry showed two missing aces. The lead was ♦10. Declarer played low but East went up with the ace anyway and returned a low diamond. South's thoughts were later captured by the *Bridge World*:

> Stayman could scarcely assume that his RHO [right-hand opponent] had had a brainstorm (which, according to Perry's later statement, was the fact) and so he decided to play for the remote chance that West, in addition to the singleton diamond with which he seemed marked, had a singleton trump. (Remember, Stayman was in only Five Spades.) So Sam [Stayman] ruffed the diamond return high and led to the trump eight.

When he led ♦K and discarded a club, however, West trumped with his second spade and fired back a club. Another 100 points for the unknowns.

ONE DIAMOND, DOUBLED AND REDOUBLED

ENGLAND, DECEMBER 1953

This deal is from the England trials before a Camrose Cup match against Northern Ireland. At one table it produced an unusual outcome.

Dealer South. Love All.

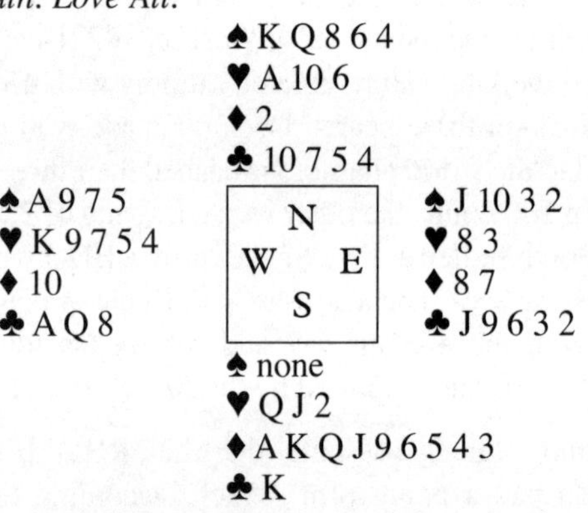

West	**North**	**East**	**South**
			1♦
Dble	Redble	All Pass	

East–West were playing – or trying to play – a system whereby a pass of a redoubled major showed weakness and a pass of a redoubled minor showed strength.

West led his singleton trump and South took the first trick and played seven more rounds of trumps. After seven discards, West was left sitting with ♠A, ♥K, ♥9, ♣A and ♣Q. South took the heart finesse and ruffed a spade (dropping the ace). He could then go across to a heart and the rest were good.

One Diamond, redoubled, six over.

Even some experts do not know that score by rote. The answer was 790 . . . I think.

TWELVE DOWN FOR A PENALTY OF 7,000

MÉGÈVE, FRANCE, 1954

This cute little teaser arose in a rubber-bridge match. How would you bid the North–South hands?

Dealer East. North–South Game.

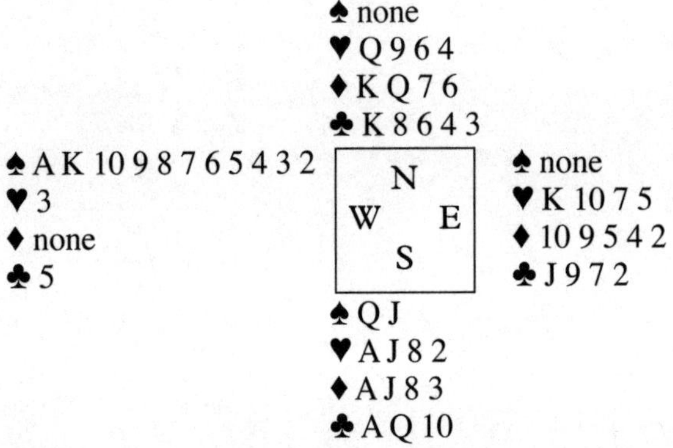

West	**North**	**East**	**South**
		Pass	1 NT
4 ♥	Dble	Pass	Pass
5 ♦	Dble	Pass	6 NT
Dble	Redble	All Pass	

Faced with psychic bidding by West, North–South were lured into an awkward contract. Not surprisingly, West led a spade, and went on to make the first eleven tricks with the suit. South retained

♦A and ♣A, while East kept the two top hearts. A small heart from West enabled East to win the last two tricks.

Twelve off, doubled, redoubled, vulnerable.

There were far better slam contracts of course. Six Clubs has a chance on a club lead, but a lead of ♠A, ruffed in dummy, overruffed by East, might have caused health problems for South. And a diamond return would have set back declarer's recovery.

Six Clubs does make if declarer has the foresight to ruff high on a spade lead, finesse ♣10, play ♣A and ♣Q, and then play on the red suits. Then East makes only one trick.

TRIO BRIDGE

USA, 1955

In most three-person bridge games, three people play against each other, competing for a dummy which may be semi-exposed (as in Towie), completely exposed or hidden. In Trio Bridge, the subject of George Coffin's *Bridge for Three* (1955), two players (North and South) play against a third (East), who partners an exposed dummy (West). South always bids first, no matter who deals, and North next. East then has to pick the correct contract from a dummy-double position. If North or South is declarer, there is no second dummy. If East wins the contract, North–South will have to sharpen up their defensive skills.

'Besides being good fun, three-handed contract affords weak players excellent and much-needed practice in their defensive play,' said George Coffin, who invented Trio Bridge in 1932. 'Because the bidding is so easy, it gives to novices much pleasure, and also trains them to size up the other hands of which only two are hidden.'

The rules for Trio Bridge, also called Triangle Bridge, are given in *The Bridge Players' Encyclopedia* under 'Three-handed Bridge'. Here is a specimen hand from a gambling game involving top players. What would you lead as South against a contract of Seven Hearts, bearing in mind that East is obviously trying to make up some lost money and that you can see the West hand before you lead?

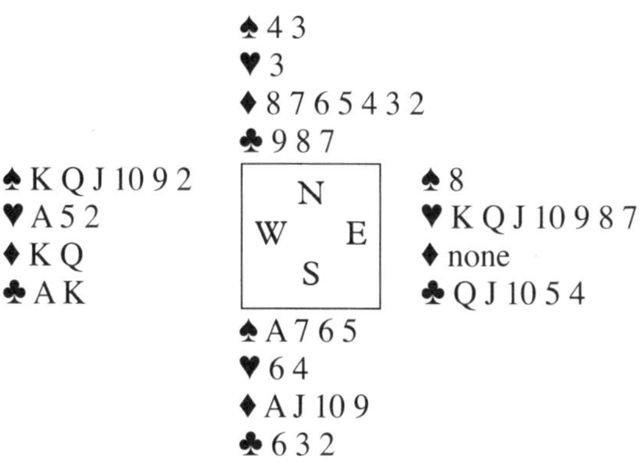

South	West	North	East
	Exposed Hand		
1♦		3♦	7♥
All Pass			

South assumed that declarer had a strong two-suiter. South could see ten spades – four in his hand and six on the table – and only six diamonds. He assumed his partner would have four, five or six diamonds for the support bid and most likely three spades. So South led ♦A and played into East's trap. The spade loser went on ♦K and Seven Hearts made, despite missing two aces.

THE MOONRAKER HAND

FICTION, 1955

Ian Fleming used the Duke of Cumberland hand (see page 2) to exercise his imagination when writing *Moonraker* (1955), one of his fourteen James Bond novels. Facing his old enemy Sir Hugo Drax, Bond rigs a pack of cards beforehand and then substitutes the pack when it is his deal. He warns his partner, 'M', that this is the crucial deal by a prearranged signal (bringing out a handkerchief).

It is the fourth rubber. Bond and his partner lead two to one, but the stakes are climbing and Bond is feigning drunkenness from the champagne. Naturally Drax fancies his chances with a 'Duke of Cumberland' powerhouse and raises the stakes still higher. The 'drunken' Bond agrees the bet and the trap is set.

Dealer South.

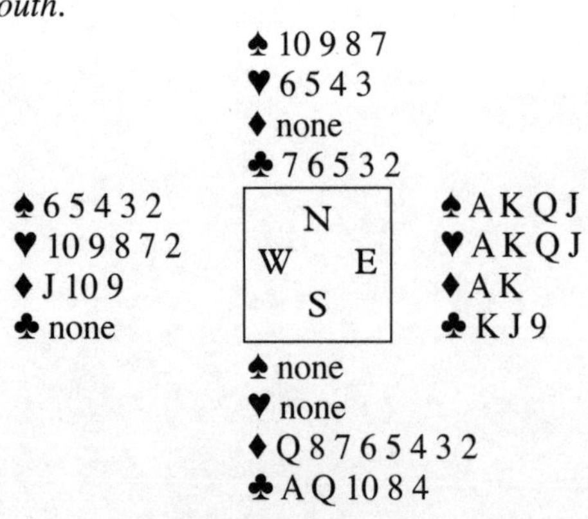

West	**North**	**East**	**South**
Meyer	*'M'*	*Drax*	*Bond*
			7 ♣
Pass	Pass	Dble	Redble
All Pass			

West led ♦J, which was ruffed in dummy. Then followed the standard sequence of finessing the clubs and ruffing the diamonds. By the third round, all the remaining diamonds were winners.

The weakness in Fleming's construction is that Drax can still bid Seven Spades, which is two off at worst. If you are thinking of setting up a hand while opponents are out of the room, there are perhaps surer deals in this book.

A RULING IN FAVOUR OF THE ERRING TEAM

ENGLAND, 1956

This was the deciding board in a mixed-teams Hubert Phillips Bowl match. It is an interesting hand in itself, but it became even more interesting when the director got involved.

Dealer South. Game All.

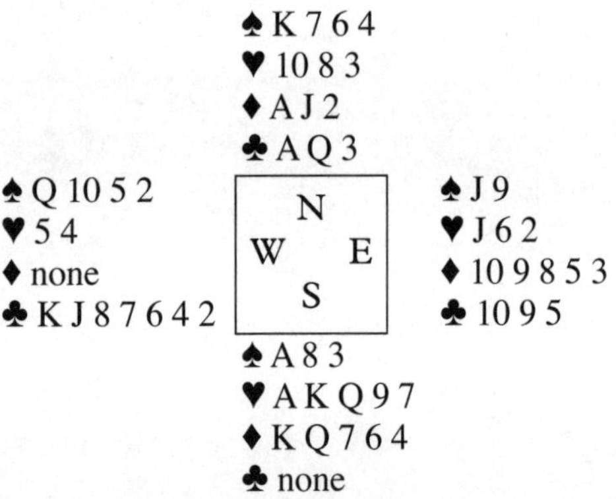

West	North	East	South
			2 ♥
Pass	3 ♥	Pass	4 NT
Pass	5 ♥	Pass	5 NT
Pass	6 ♦	Pass	7 ♥
All Pass			

West led a spade and declarer took the trick with dummy's king.

Everything now seems to depend on a favourable trump split. Declarer cashed ♥A and then continued with the king. To her relief both opponents followed suit.

'There they are,' said declarer, laying down her remaining ten cards.

But East was unhappy with the claim.

'I naturally play another round of trumps,' spluttered South.

'Naturally,' echoed her partner.

'Director,' said East.

The laws at the time were strict. When she made the claim, South had not indicated that she was drawing the last trump. The ruling was therefore that she was not allowed to lead trumps (unless there was no alternative).

This is where the hand became really strange – this ruling actually helped declarer. First let us see what actually happened.

Declarer, not permitted to lead hearts, turned to diamonds – ace, jack in dummy, king, queen in her hand. Then the last diamond was ruffed in dummy. She led ♣A, discarding a spade, then returned to hand with ♠A. Declarer now had only hearts in her hand, and was therefore allowed to play trumps. Grand slam made.

Because of the director's ruling against her, South had found the only way to make the grand slam. But consider what would have happened if she had drawn the last trump. Was there any way to make the contract?

She could not set up the thirteenth spade, as they split four–two. She could not squeeze West in spades and clubs, because, having used ♠K on the first trick, there were not enough entries.

In such strange ways can matches be decided.

THE ZERO–ZERO FIT

USA, 1956

A contract of Five Spades with a zero–zero spade fit made a top score on the following hand.

Nikos Sarantakos resurrected the story for *Bridge Plus* (October 2000). As he says, 'You may suspect the veracity of this deal, and indeed its documentation is deficient. We know no names, only that it was played in a Washington tournament in 1956.'

Dealer West. Love All.

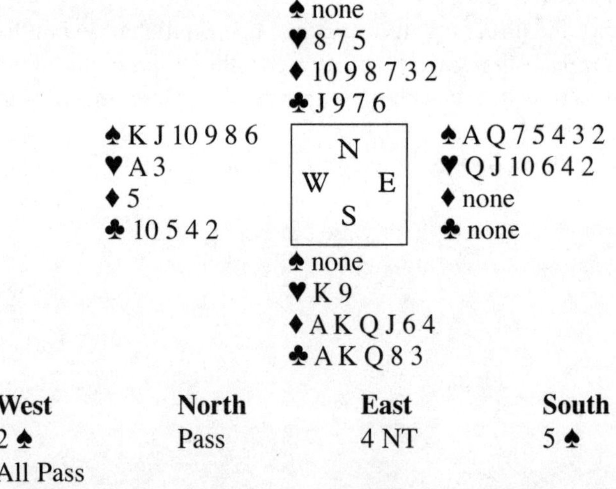

West	**North**	**East**	**South**
2 ♠	Pass	4 NT	5 ♠
All Pass			

West opened a weak Two Spades, and East immediately went to Blackwood. South cue-bid the spade void and then, as Sarantakos wrote, 'For some reason or other, after that no one saw fit to make any call other than pass.'

Presumably West felt pushed too far to respond Six Spades, North misinterpreted South's bid and East saw penalty points flashing in his mind, worried that a double would allow South to take refuge in a minor. As it happens, East–West can make Six Spades safely and even Seven Spades (with the friendly heart finesse). What seems at first sight to be North–South's 30th-best contract actually works out well.

West led his singleton diamond and then had two shocks: the first was sight of dummy; and the second was partner's ruff. Defence made all the tricks. Eleven off for 550 points. A good top, provided all the other East–Wests found their slam in spades, although Seven Diamonds was a good sacrifice.

THE STRANGE LEAD

COMO, ITALY, 1958

And now for the category of strange leads. The judges have had a hard time deciding on the strangest, but Robert Ewen included this one in the 'Opening Lead Hall of Fame' chapter of his book *Opening Leads* (1970). It may not seem especially fantastic today, but it caused a sensation at the 1958 Bermuda Bowl. This was Board 40 in the final between Italy and North America. Pietro Forquet of Italy was sitting West.

Dealer East. Love All.

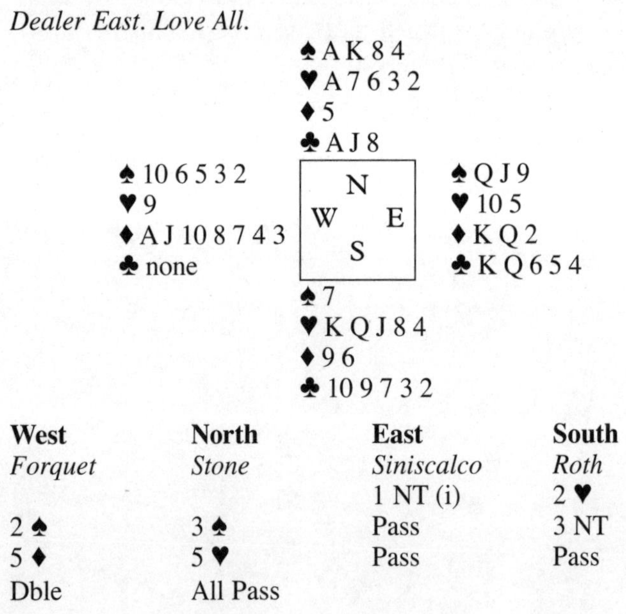

West	**North**	**East**	**South**
Forquet	*Stone*	*Siniscalco*	*Roth*
		1 NT (i)	2 ♥
2 ♠	3 ♠	Pass	3 NT
5 ♦	5 ♥	Pass	Pass
Dble	All Pass		

(i) Twelve–fifteen points and five clubs or a balanced sixteen–seventeen points

Forquet led ♦3. His partner won the king and then returned a low club for Forquet to use his only trump. Then East sat back and waited for a club trick. One off.

In the other room the Italian declarer made Five Diamonds.

'Suppose West leads ♦A and shifts to a spade,' writes Ewen,

> Dummy wins and a low spade is ruffed, South cashes two high trumps and ruffs his last diamond in dummy, and cashes ♠K (pitching a club) and ruffs a spade. Declarer then leads a low club to dummy's eight, and East wins but is forced to make a most unhappy choice. He must either concede a ruff and discard or lead into North's club tenace, allowing declarer to bring home his contract.

Victor Mollo commented on the hand in *The Other Side of Bridge* (1984): 'Given the bidding and the system, it was an inspired, but perfectly logical, lead. To this day the Americans haven't forgiven him for it and there were dark hints of hanky-panky at the time.'

TWELVE OF A SUIT

SAILING HOME FROM INDIA, 1959

You pick up your hand and open out the cards. Maybe you sort your hand into suits and card order as you go. Or maybe you can see what the whole hand is worth without sorting the cards. Maybe you never sort your cards and keep your partner on tenterhooks when delivering dummy: *Only one spade?... Oh, and one heart... Oh, another spade... three spades... two hearts...*

'Thank you, partner. Very exciting.'

Whatever your method of assessing your holding, there is that once-in-a-lifetime hand that requires hardly any sorting. The twelve-card suit is tricky only in that it raises a perverse question: which one is missing?

In a letter to *Bridge* (Summer 2001), Joan Bradley of Grantham, Lincolnshire, recalled playing bridge on the MV *Caledonia* during a trip from India to England. It is almost statutory for a book of strange bridge hands to include at least one game played on a ship, if only to pay homage to the old joke about cross-ruffing on a rough crossing.

On board MV *Caledonia*, Joan Bradley reached the final of a knock-out competition in which entrants drew for partners and each round of the tournament consisted of three rubbers.

'We were one game all in the final rubber,' she wrote 42 years later, 'but a quick glance at the scorecard made me realise that the only way we could win was to get a slam in the final game.'

Then she and her partner picked up these hands.

♠ K Q J 10 x x x x x x x
♥ A
♦ K
♣ none

♠ none
♥ K Q J 10 9 8 7 6 5 4 3 2
♦ none
♣ 3

West	**North**	**East**	**South**
			Joan Bradley
Pass	4 NT	Pass	6 ♥
Pass	6 ♠	All Pass	

They had agreed to play Gerber to ask for aces, so Four No-trumps was a little puzzling. South took it as natural.

Six Spades was one off. Seven Hearts would have been perfect.

THREE NO-TRUMPS (REDOUBLED)

LONDON, DECEMBER 1960

The internationals Bob and Jim Sharples were identical twins and sometimes opponents could not tell North from South. They were both Grand Masters. They represented Great Britain together and were Gold-Cup winning partners (1962), Masters Pairs winners (1950) and European Championships runners-up (1958). They were also jointly responsible for conventions.

Despite the Sharples twins' parallel paths, however, there was one experience that was solely Bob's. He was playing with the bridge journalist G C H Fox one day at a London club when they defended ruthlessly to set a redoubled contract of Three No-trumps by nine tricks.

Dealer West. East–West Game.

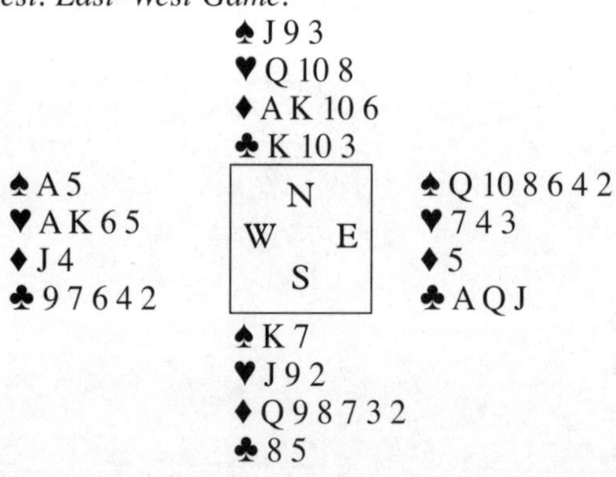

West	**North**	**East**	**South**
Sharples		*Fox*	
Pass	1 ♦	1 ♠	2 NT
3 ♠	3 NT	Pass	Pass
Dble	Redble	All Pass	

South's bid of Two No-trumps was a gambling bid in the hope of a spade lead to the king, six diamond tricks and a late scramble for the eighth. It is not the first time that a pair have strayed into Three No-trumps on a combined total of nineteen points, but rarely has a declarer been punished so severely.

West led ♥A and then switched to ♣4, which was won by East's jack. Defence's third trick was a heart to West's king. West returned ♣9, suggesting a spade lead. Fox won ♣Q and unblocked by cashing ♣A. Then he led a spade. South played ♠K, which lost to the ace. West cashed two more clubs and then led a spade to East's five spade winners.

Thirteen tricks to defence – two hearts, five clubs and six spades. The penalty was 3,400 points.

It would make for a good caption competition: what did North say to South after Three No-trumps (redoubled) had gone nine off?

Good job we weren't vulnerable, partner.
Maybe we should have been in diamonds.
Three No-trumps is a good bid but not on this hand.

Or maybe North turned to his left and addressed Fox thus: 'I would like to buy a copy of your book, *Sound Bidding at Contract*, for my partner.'

Had South looked at the book, he would have found the paragraph on weak limit-bids supporting a partner's suit: five to nine high-card points and four in your partner's bid suit.

THE EARTHQUAKE OF SÃO PAULO

BRAZIL, 1961

The French team were on their way to Buenos Aires for the 1961 Bermuda Bowl when they stopped in São Paulo, Brazil, to play some friendly matches. This hand was talked about for years. It was dubbed 'the earthquake of São Paulo'.

Dealer South. Game all.

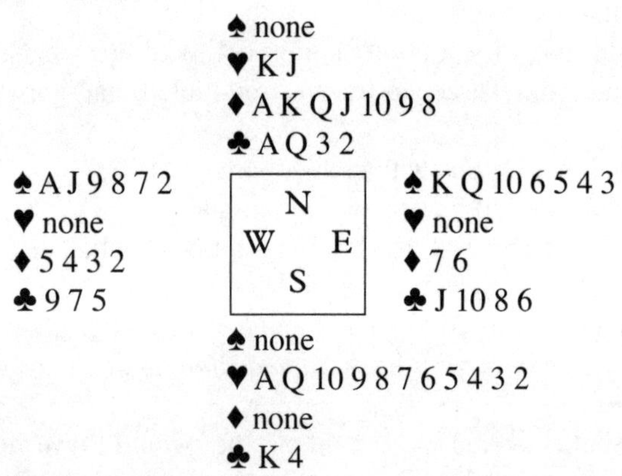

In one room, when Brazil sat North–South, they bid and made Seven Hearts to score 2,210 points.

In the other room, where the French South passed on the first round of bidding, a strange development occurred.

West	**North**	**East**	**South**
			Pass
Pass	2 ♣	2 ♠	7 ♥
Pass	Pass	7 ♠	Pass
Pass	7 NT	Dble	All Pass

West hesitated before passing Seven Hearts, so the French called the director when East bid Seven Spades. The bid was allowed and the French North responded with an emotional Seven No-trumps. Defence won seven spade tricks off the top and scored 2,000 points. The swing was 4,210 points, which amounted to 25 IMPs (on the scoring system of the day).

Incidentally, the French won the match.

FACT OR FICTION?

A HAND FROM BRIDGE LITERATURE, 1961

Bridge fiction is as old as bridge. In the 1920s and 1930s, bridge addicts occasionally dragged themselves away from the table to watch theatre shows like E Kidder's *The Bridge Party* (1927) and W T Gregory's *As the Ladies Play It* (1930). Somerset Maugham's classic short-story 'Three Fat Women of Antibes', written in 1933, was set around bridge, and a novel by B Russell Herts, *Grand Slam* (1932), was turned into a Hollywood film. Herts tells how a Russian waiter is called in to make up a fourth at bridge. Naturally the waiter turns out to be an expert.

Other characters from the 1930s include Hubert Phillips's Mr Playbetter and George Coffin's Samuel Pitt. Skid Simon later introduced a stereotypical bridge quartet – Mrs Guggenheim, Mr Smug, Futile Willie and the Unlucky Expert – in *Cut for Partners* and Victor Mollo developed this idea further. Mollo's cast of animals formed the basis for a long-running magazine series and several books – *Bridge in the Menagerie*, *Bridge in the Fourth Dimension*, *Masters and Monsters* and *Destiny at Bay*. The Hideous Hog and his animal friends play at the Griffins Club, watched by the senior kibitzer, Oscar the Owl. You have to admire the creativity of a man like Mollo, who once wrote an article called 'Leading from a Void'.

The post-war period also brought novels like Hilda Boden's *Bridge Club* (1952) and B H Friedman's *Yarborough* (1965). The latter, a tale of bridge, sex, drugs and rock 'n' roll, follows a lonely bridge professional as he tries to answer the question: Why am I here? ('Some day, he thought, he would name a hand after Hull, one in which all the cards were *above* a nine: a Hull, fate dealing a Yarborough upside down.') Ewart Kempson, editor of *Bridge Magazine*, seemed to think that *Yarborough* was as pointless as a hand of that name. 'I suppose I'm old-fashioned,' he wrote in his review. 'It made me feel sick.'

More recent fictional diversions include Frank Thomas's *Sherlock Holmes: Bridge Detective* (1973), while the prolific David Bird has produced not only his 'Abbot' series, featuring the monks of St Titus, but also *The Bridge Adventures of Robin Hood* and *Robin Hood's Bridge Memoirs*. The father-and-son team Phillip and Robert King have written a series of parodies with hard-boiled titles: *Contract Killers*; *Play it Again, Slam*; *Farewell, My Dummy*; and *Your Deal, Mr Bond*. In *Bridge Literature* (1993), Nick Smith offers several adaptations of classic literature, including a chapter about Julius Caesar called 'Beware the Five of Hearts!'. Smith introduces Caesar as 'Pons Maximus, Bridge Supremo of all Rome and a modest empire to boot'.

Mainstream writers occasionally turn their minds to plots with bridge settings. The most widely known are Agatha Christie's *Cards on the Table* (1936) and Roald Dahl's short story about cheating, 'My Lady Love, My Dove', published in *Someone Like You* (1953). Other writers make passing reference to the game. Ian Fleming does this with a hand in *Moonraker* (1955), which is featured in this book (see page 114), and Sue Grafton has a quick sideswipe in *B is for Burglar* (1986): 'I didn't think Marty Grice had been killed for messing up a small slam, but with bridge players one can never be sure.'

E R Cole and James Edwards provided an anthology of thirteen pieces of bridge fiction in *Grand Slam* (1975). Only Ring Lardner could describe an old lady as 'venerable' at game-all and have a character say, 'It's a game you can't learn in a minute.' Lardner's husband and wife characters argue about whether they should accept a bridge invitation even though the host and hostess may be very good players. 'I don't care if they're Lenz's mother-in-law,' says the more socially climbing of the two.

Also in the Cole and Edwards collection, George Kaufman offers his theory of 'The Great Kibitzers' Strike of 1926', a story which first appeared in the *New Yorker* (1949), and Don Von Elsner's sleuth, Jake Winkman, is the investigator hero of 'The Man Who Played Too Well': 'He and Jeanne hit a small slam that was cold but hard to reach, and followed it up with a grand slam that was tighter than an actor's girdle.'

More recently, in the 1990s, another crime-fiction writer, Susan Moody, created a murder-solving bridge professional as her heroine. We see little of Cassandra Swann's bridge expertise in these novels but when a hand does appear (about once a book in the earlier novels) it is usually a strange one. The titles are very recognisable – *Takeout Double* (1993), *Grand Slam* (1994), *King of Hearts* (1995), *Doubled in Spades* (1996), *Sacrifice Bid* (1997) and *Dummy Hand* (1999).

The line between fact and fiction can be very slim. Some authors use real hands set around fictional characters and others invent hands. The hand below is taken from Hubert Phillips's *Bridge is Only a Game* (1961). Phillips invented the hand for a previous book called *Complete Contract Bridge* (1948). His narrator is Fanny, about whom the author says, 'It would not be slanderous to describe her as a minx.' She is sitting South, partnering Julian (Eton and King's), 'who has played for Cambridge against Oxford'.

Dealer West.

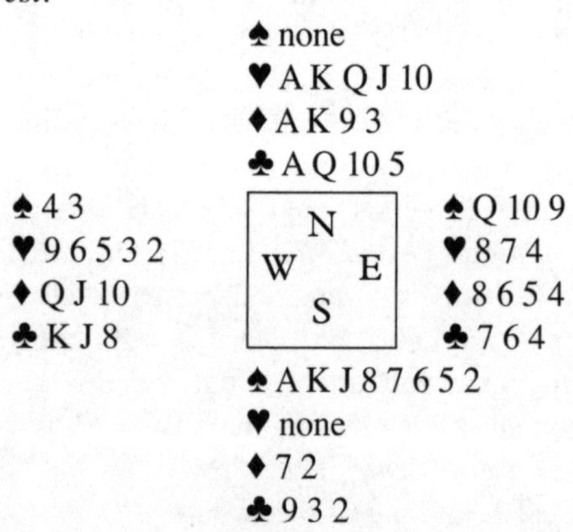

West	**North**	**East**	**South**
Pippin	*Julian*	*Tigger*	*Fanny*
Pass	2 ♣	Pass	2 ♠
Pass	3 ♥	Pass	3 ♠
Pass	4 ♦	Pass	6 ♠
Pass	7 ♠	All Pass	

Julian has put Fanny into an optimistic contract of Seven Spades. She is playing against Pippin ('the putative French count who regards Fanny as his most promising pupil') and Pippin's girlfriend Tigger ('who has everything'). Pippin leads ♥9 and Fanny goes into a huddle.

Ah, Fanny concludes, to play this hand I have to assume the clubs break three–three, Tigger has three spades to the queen and Pippin has ♣K and ♣J.

'OK,' she says, after the long pause. 'Seconds out of the ring.'

She trumps her winning ♥10 with a low spade, then plays ♣9 and overtakes it with the ten. Dummy's ♥J is trumped and then she returns to dummy by finessing ♣K. Next she trumps ♥Q and returns to dummy with ♣A. Dummy's ♥K is ruffed, with Tigger throwing a diamond, so Fanny enters dummy with a top diamond. Having got an exact count of opponents' hands, she comes back to hand by ruffing ♥A, returns to dummy with another top diamond and finesses Tigger's ♠Q.

Seven Spades with a quintuple Grand Coup. What a heroine.

A SLAM EITHER WAY

ENGLAND, MARCH 1962

It is said that one hand in fifteen has potential for a small slam, but how often does a hand lend itself to the chance of a slam either way? This example shows how a team of four players of international standard explored a rare opportunity.

Dealer South. East–West Game.

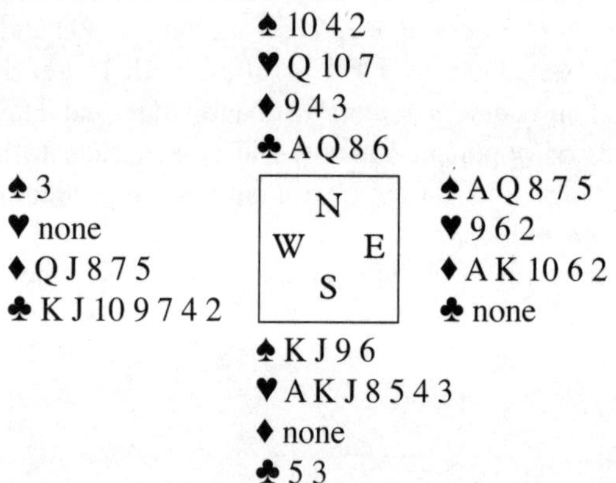

Table 1

West	North	East	South
			4 ♥
Pass	Pass	4 ♠	Dble
5 ♣	Dble	5 ♦	Pass
Pass	5 ♥	Dble	Pass
6 ♦	Pass	Pass	6 ♥
Pass	Pass	Dble	All Pass

Table 2

West	**North**	**East**	**South**
			1 ♥
Pass	2 ♥	Dble	4 ♥
5 ♣	Dble	5 ♦	5 ♥
6 ♦	Pass	Pass	Dble
All Pass			

Ah, the difference a bid decision can make. One South doubled Six Diamonds, the other bid Six Hearts.

At Table 1, West failed to lead a club and defence lost a ruffing opportunity. South guessed that East had a two-suiter and at least two trumps, so the only loser in reality was ♠A.

At Table 2, there were several ways to play the hand. It is possible to set up two club winners, plus ♠A, and use all ten trumps.

A GRAND SLAM AGAINST ALL ODDS

USA, 1963

This hand turned up in a minor tournament.

Dealer South. North–South Game.

	♠A K J ♥Q 9 3 ♦9 8 7 4 3 ♣K 9	
♠Q 7 6 5 ♥2 ♦none ♣Q J 8 7 6 5 3 2	N W E S	♠9 8 4 3 2 ♥K 8 7 6 5 ♦A 10 ♣10
	♠10 ♥A J 10 4 ♦K Q J 6 5 2 ♣A 4	

West	**North**	**East**	**South**
			1 ♦
Pass	3 ♦	Pass	3 ♥
4 NT	5 ♦	5 ♠	6 ♦
6 ♠	Pass	Pass	7 ♦
		Dble	7 NT

At one point in the auction, South bid a hopeless Seven Diamonds when he could have doubled Six Spades (which goes off by several). Kibitzers must have been wondering if South would retain his partner at the end of the hand. But sometimes everything turns out all right in the end. This lucky South made a grand slam after all.

East rescued South by doubling Seven Diamonds *out of turn*. Then he compounded his error by leading ♦A *when it wasn't his lead*.

The tournament director arrived at the table, heard the parties and made a ruling: West was barred from the bidding; South could bid again; and ♦A was a penalty card that had to be played at the first legal opportunity.

South bid Seven No-trumps and that concluded the bidding.

Seven No-trumps looks as impossible as Seven Diamonds, doesn't it?

Well, actually, South was obliged to discard ♦A on the second round of clubs, and Seven No-trumps cruised home with a trick to spare (if that is possible).

There are other cases of players making seemingly impossible contracts. A man once made Seven Hearts when missing ♥A. One opponent held back the missing ace and did not realise that he had fourteen cards until it came to the thirteenth trick and his partner showed out.

PASSING WITH OVER TWENTY POINTS – LESSON 2

PARIS, 1964

The Paris trials were held to select the French team for the 1964 Olympiad. Spectators following this hand on the Bridgerama screen were baffled by East's action.

Dealer East.

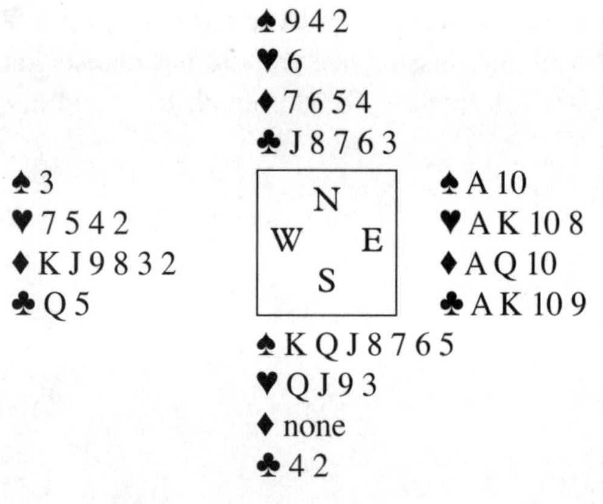

West	**North**	**East**	**South**
		Pass	4 ♠
All Pass			

Everyone was bemused. How could East pass twice with 24 points? Why were East–West not playing the hand in Six Diamonds or Six No-trumps, both of which make?

The answer was simple. East was still holding his hand from the previous board. He had been so caught up in that previous hand, he had failed to return it to the board and collect the next one. In fact, the four players had done well to find a contract from a pack containing fewer than 30 points.

Most bridge players have some experience of confusing two packs of cards. I remember one night when four of us were playing rubber bridge. Our two packs had the same picture on the back and they differed only in that one pack had a gold trim and the other a silver trim. My right-hand opponent doubled my partner's Three Clubs and then threw his hand down.

'We're not playing this one,' he said.

'I've got thirteen,' I said.

The other two players confirmed that they had thirteen. Then we looked at the hand on the table. Six clubs and two of them were aces.

The dealer had obviously brushed the top card off the other pack and it was another ♣A. We all agreed that it was worth a double.

ALL BUT IMPOSSIBLE

RICHMOND, SURREY, AUGUST 1964

This unbelievable hand made the front page of the *Daily Mail* and the inside pages of every other British newspaper. It was covered on BBC news bulletins and the players were hooked up for a trans-atlantic interview with CBS in New York City.

The hand was dealt at the Richmond Community Centre on 25 August 1964 and one of the participants, David Rex-Taylor, wrote an account for *Bridge Magazine* (October 1964):

> The pack (a used one) had been shuffled by Mrs Lilian Hennion, of St Margarets Road, Twickenham, who has a reputation for particularly thorough shuffling. Mrs Phoebe Dawson, of Lavender Hill, Clapham Junction, cut the cards. The deal was made by Mrs Edith Gyde of Mount Ararat Road, Richmond, the club's hostess. The writer (of Whitton Waye, Hounslow) was the dealer's partner. Among others present during the deal was Mr T G Tai of Kew.
>
> Having dealt, Mrs Gyde picked up thirteen clubs, and involuntarily gasped. In almost the same instant, Mrs Hennion, on dealer's left, seeing her thirteen diamonds, said, 'This is extraordinary, I really must show you my hand.' We all exposed our 'dream' hands with astonishment, for the miracle was that not only did we each have a complete suit, but the cards had actually been dealt in order of rank around the table.

Most experts are very suspicious of reports of four one-suiters. Indeed, one case reported in a London club turned out to be a hoax.

A spectator had substituted a prepared pack for the correctly shuffled pack that was waiting to be dealt. Consequently the players believed the deal was legitimate.

The Richmond hand was the sixth report of four players being each dealt a complete suit in the same deal – one in Scotland, one in Wales and two in England. One was reported to *Bridge Magazine* (June 1938) by Peter Bruff after its occurrence at the Woodstock Hotel, London N5.

I have no record of the bidding at the Richmond Community Centre. I assume everyone kowtowed to Seven Spades. What do you think? Is it really worth swotting up on this type of hand in case we get dealt one?

ANOTHER MIRACLE HAND

INDIA, APRIL 1965

Ewart Kempson, the editor of *Bridge Magazine*, received an envelope with an Indian stamp. Inside was a note from the captain of the all-India bridge team saying that each of the six signatories of the enclosed affidavit was a man of the highest integrity. The document had a suitably legalistic tone.

Kempson printed the statement without comment under the heading 'Another Miracle Hand'. He left his readers to judge for themselves. I shall do likewise. The statement read as follows:

> We, S N Sahai, K S Dassania, R T I Mohan and B R Mehta, were playing rubber bridge at the residence of S N Sahai, a retired judge of the Allahabad High Court, on the afternoon of 28 April 1965.
>
> On the second deal, the cards, which had been in use for a number of days, were shuffled by S N Sahai. They were cut by B R Mehta and then dealt by K S Dassania. Dassania had thirteen hearts, Sahai thirteen diamonds, Mohan thirteen clubs and Mehta thirteen spades. Dassania called Seven Hearts, Sahai and Mohan had to pass, and Mehta called Seven Spades.
>
> Moti Babu, alias Radhika Prasad Agarwal, a prominent Allahabad businessman and national bridge player, and Sachchidanand Sahai, an advocate of the High Court, were present watching the game when the miracle deal occurred.

The affidavit was signed by K S Dassania (vice-president of the Northern India Bridge Association), S N Sahai (a retired judge from the Allahabad High Court), B R Mehta (president of the Northern India Bridge Association), R T I Mohan (as retired Additional Commissioner), Radhika Prasad Agarwal and Sachchidanand Sahai.

THE BUENOS AIRES AFFAIR (1) – CASE FOR THE PROSECUTION

BUENOS AIRES, ARGENTINA, 1965

Four teams competed for the 1965 Bermuda Bowl World Championships – Italy (holders), North America (American champions), Great Britain (European champions) and Argentina (representing South America) – but a furore ensued when two British players, Terence Reese and Boris Schapiro, were accused of cheating.

It was alleged that Reese and Schapiro used finger signals to transmit information about their heart holdings. In those days it was common for Bermuda Bowl players to hold their cards above their heads so that spectators could see the cards. Two members of the North America team, backed by Alan Truscott, bridge editor of the *New York Times*, claimed that Reese and Schapiro used a system of signals when holding up the cards. One visible finger showed a singleton heart, two closed fingers indicated two hearts, two spread fingers meant five hearts, three closed fingers was three hearts, three spread fingers six hearts and so on.

In his book on the Buenos Aires Affair, *The Great Bridge Scandal* (1967), Alan Truscott documents what he saw as the evidence against Reese and Schapiro. Truscott was an authority on the game. He was British by birth and had represented Great Britain before moving to the United States in 1962. In Buenos Aires, he was approached by suspicious North American players and officials to act as an independent witness.

Having been told about the finger-code system, Truscott joined a number of people who studied the behaviour of Reese and Schapiro during matches. They included two North American players, Jay

Becker and Dorothy Hayden, John Gerber (North America's captain), Ralph Swimer (the British non-playing captain) and Geoffrey Butler (chairman of the British Bridge League). Equipped with a coding system – 3d meant three visible fingers with a drooping fourth – the group found the finger signal corresponded to the expected heart holding in 58 of 65 hands. Reese and Schapiro returned to a normal card-holding grip when play started.

When faced with this evidence, Ralph Swimer conceded the Great Britain–Argentina match, which Britain had won 380-184, and he also conceded the Great Britain–North America match, which was 288–242 to the British with twenty boards to play. Swimer decided that only Konstam, Harrison-Gray, Rose and Flint would be considered for selection for the remaining boards in the Italy match.

Reese and Schapiro immediately publicly denied the accusations, but Ralph Swimer later reported a private conversation with Schapiro in which the player allegedly confessed. On the last day of the Championships, however, the executive committee of the World Bridge Federation voted 10–0 (with one abstention) that Reese and Schapiro were guilty of using illegal signals. It was not the first time Schapiro had been in trouble. He and Kenneth Konstam had both been suspended for three matches in 1949 after they had spoken to each other in the bar during a match against Italy. Schapiro had not been playing in that match but was part of the team. There had also been previous accusations that Reese and Schapiro had developed some sort of code based on the height at which they were holding the cards and the desired lead or the number of points.

The Buenos Aires evidence was turned over to the British Bridge League, who arranged for an independent inquiry under Sir John Foster, a prominent judge (see page 145, 'Case for the Defence'). Meanwhile, Alan Truscott documented eight suspicious hands where he felt the heart holding was known and play was adapted accordingly. Here is one from the Italy match.

'This psychic bid of Two Hearts by Schapiro may be unique in the literature of the game,' he wrote in *The Great Bridge Scandal*. 'I cannot recall seeing anything like it in the past twenty years. The reason is not difficult to see: in an honest partnership the risks far outweigh the prospects of gain.'

Truscott claimed that the bid of Two Hearts could only be made with the knowledge that Reese had two hearts and therefore would not support the suit.

Dealer East. North–South Game.

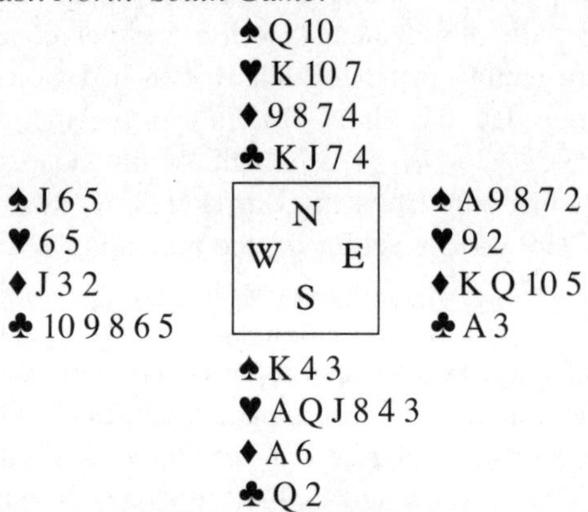

♠Q 10
♥K 10 7
♦9 8 7 4
♣K J 7 4

♠J 6 5
♥6 5
♦J 3 2
♣10 9 8 6 5

♠A 9 8 7 2
♥9 2
♦K Q 10 5
♣A 3

♠K 4 3
♥A Q J 8 4 3
♦A 6
♣Q 2

West	**North**	**East**	**South**
Reese	*Forquet*	*Schapiro*	*Garozzo*
		1 ♠	Dble
Pass	2 ♣	2 ♥	Pass
2 ♠	Pass	Pass	2 NT
All Pass			

Reese led ♠5 and Garozzo made eight tricks. In the other room, the British pair made Four Hearts for a swing of ten IMPs.

THE BUENOS AIRES AFFAIR (2) – CASE FOR THE DEFENCE

BUENOS AIRES, ARGENTINA, 1965

'The Turkish cigarette is cocked in the thin lips until it points towards the ear; the sharp features are marked with supercilious disdain; the long, nervous fingers flick out a card without use of the thumb; and an indecipherable scrawl records the score.'

This action profile was of Terence Reese, Bermuda Bowl winner in 1955 and one of the accused in the 1965 Buenos Aires cheating allegations (see page 142). Reese was also a prolific author, presenter of the radio series *Bridge on the Air* and editor of *British Bridge World.* His acerbic wit occasionally produced memorable lines: for example, 'She is a woman who calls a spade Two Spades.'

Ten months after the British Bridge League had arranged for an independent inquiry under Sir John Foster, Terence Reese and Boris Schapiro were found 'not guilty' of cheating at the Bermuda Bowl. Foster found 'reasonable doubt' for two reasons. First, the British players had not deviated from their normal pattern of play. Second, one of the North American officials had already withdrawn his accusation. Foster concluded that the relationship between the heart holding and the number of fingers was purely coincidental.

Nevertheless, it meant the end of a distinguished international career which had seen Reese play for Great Britain in teams which had won four European Championships and one World Championship. He continued his career as an author and eventually contributed over 80 books to bridge, a body of work that allows him to be judged in the highest class as a player and a bridge writer. His book on the Buenos Aires Affair, *Story of an Accusation* (1966), is one of bridge's best reads, a mix of hand analysis, descriptions of bridge rivalries and behind-the-scenes tales of international team selection.

In Reese and Schapiro's favour, the condemning decision of the World Bridge Federation came at a hastily called committee meeting which gave Reese and Schapiro little time to construct a defence. And, as Reese said at the meeting, 'How does one rebut this sort of accusation?'

Rixi Markus was one who doubted the legitimacy of the allegations, as she explained in *A Vulnerable Game*:

> I could not believe the accusation because, in the first place, the method alleged struck me as quite ridiculous. If you are going to pass illegal signals to your partner, much the best code would indicate the lead you desire. If Reese and Schapiro had intended to cheat, they would surely have been capable of doing so more productively. Moreover, Reese and Schapiro were not only the best pair ever to have represented Great Britain, they had probably been, before the rise of the Italian Blue Team, the best pair in the world. Yet their supposed signals had been observed during the match against Argentina, much the weakest team.

In *Story of an Accusation*, Reese does not consider all of Truscott's evidence, but that may be because Reese's book came out first. Shortly after the 1965 Bermuda Bowl, Reese featured this hand – Board 26 vs. Italy – in an article for *Bridge Magazine* (September 1965). He said, 'To judge from the publicity given to this deal in the New York papers, you might think it was the most remarkable auction of the year.'

Dealer East. North–South Game.

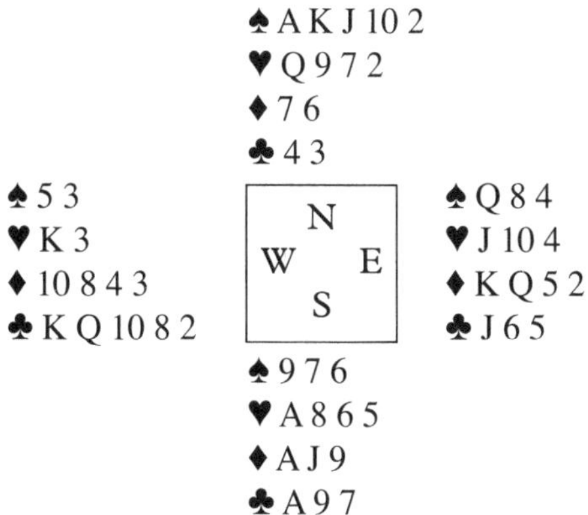

West	**North**	**East**	**South**
Garozzo	*Reese*	*Forquet*	*Schapiro*
		Pass	1 ♣
Pass	1 ♠	Pass	1 NT
Pass	2 NT	Pass	3 ♥
Pass	4 ♥	All Pass	

Reese claimed that there was nothing unusual about the British bidding. He offered three reasons for this: (i) Four Hearts actually went down; (ii) the Italians in the other room also bid to Four Hearts; and (iii) if South knew his partner had four hearts he could have opened One Heart without attracting any criticism.

Reese pointed out that Truscott had drawn attention to eight hands where he felt that the heart holding had affected the bidding, but that was only eight out of the 198 that Reese and Schapiro had played together in the 1965 Bermuda Bowl.

THE PREDICTABLY UNPREDICTABLE JOHN COLLINGS (1)

OSTEND, BELGIUM, SEPTEMBER 1965

Following the Buenos Aires Affair, and the suspensions of Terence Reese and Boris Schapiro, the British team turned to youth for the 1965 European Championships. Jonathan Cansino and John Collings were selected as the team's top pair after their success at the trials.

'Collings and Cansino were outstanding,' wrote Harold Franklin in *Bridge Magazine*, 'though a most predictable feature of their game continues to be its unpredictability.'

John Collings, at his most unpredictable in the 1960s, would be an obvious choice for a British Hall of Fame of Strange Hands. In *Bridge My Way* (1991), Zia Mahmood called Collings perhaps the greatest natural player of all time. Zia attributes one legendary story to Collings, although the tale is told of other players. Apparently Collings would sometimes pass distributional hands and then enter the bidding more spectacularly later, hoping to be doubled. One time it misfired. He sat with three singletons and ten spades to the ace, king, queen and jack. The hand was passed out.

'Did you have anything, partner?' asked Collings.

'Just three aces.'

Collings and Cansino played very well during the 1965 European Championships and Great Britain finished fourth out of eighteen. They beat West Germany 102–43 (6–0 Victory Points), but Ewart Kempson, the non-playing captain, was none too pleased. His advice at half-time, when Britain led by 30 IMPs, was, 'Steady bridge down the middle, boys.' And then came this.

Dealer West. East–West Game.

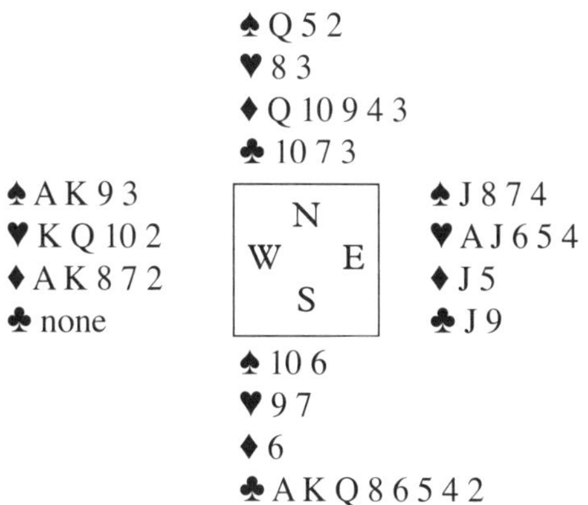

West	**North**	**East**	**South**
	Cansino		*Collings*
2♣	Pass	2♥	4♠
5 NT	7♠	Pass	Pass
Dble	All Pass		

When the German East responded positively to a game-forcing Two Clubs, John Collings decided on a psychic Four Spades. His partner, holding some spade support, bid to Seven Spades so that East–West would have no chance of finding a contract of Seven No-trumps. Unfortunately that took away Collings's refuge of Seven Clubs. West's double was inevitable.

West led ♦A and followed with ♥2 to East's ace. The return of ♣9 was ruffed by West. West led ♠9. At this point, some players, collapsing under the strain of playing a ridiculous contract, might let ♠9 run in a futile attempt to set up some sort of spade trick. Instead Collings played the queen, then ruffed a diamond and eventually made a diamond.

In the other room, the British pair bid to Six Hearts but the Germans sacrificed in Seven Clubs. Britain's 900 points failed to cancel out the 2,800 lost by Cansino and Collings.

THE PREDICTABLY UNPREDICTABLE JOHN COLLINGS (2)

ENGLAND, 1960s

It was during a game of rubber bridge that John Collings 'made one of the most remarkable hands in history', according to *Daily Telegraph* bridge correspondent Tony Forrester in *Vintage Forrester* (1998).

Dealer North. North–South Game.

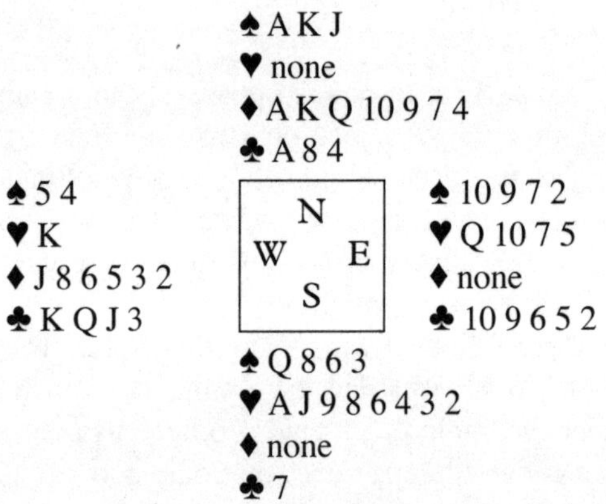

West	**North**	**East**	**South**
			Collings
	2♣	Pass	2♥
Pass	4 NT	Pass	5♦
Pass	7♦	Pass	Pass
Dble	Pass	Pass	7♥
Dble	All Pass		

When ♣K was led, South won with dummy's ace and led ♦A. East trumped with the five and South overruffed. He went across to ♠A and led ♦K. East ruffed low. Declarer overruffed and returned to dummy with a spade to the king. When ♦Q was led, East ruffed low for the third time. South overruffed again and laid down ♥A. The two outstanding trump honours fell in a heap and John Collings claimed the rest.

'We were lucky trumps broke, partner,' Collings said.

There is no record of what West said to East. Maybe it was the old maxim about not ruffing tricks when your trumps were winners anyway.

PLAYING AGAINST GENIUS

MAJORCA, OCTOBER 1967

Amy Baird wrote up this hand for *Bridge Magazine* (January 1968) because she would never forget the experience of being outthought at the bridge table by the great Italian player Giorgio Belladonna. The date was engraved on Amy Baird's mind for ever – Monday 16 October 1967.

The occasion was the Teams of Four Championship in the International Festival of Bridge. The hand is included here as a testimony to those strange hands where we think we are in control and then an opponent upstages us. (Or maybe such hands are not so strange to some of us.)

Dealer West.

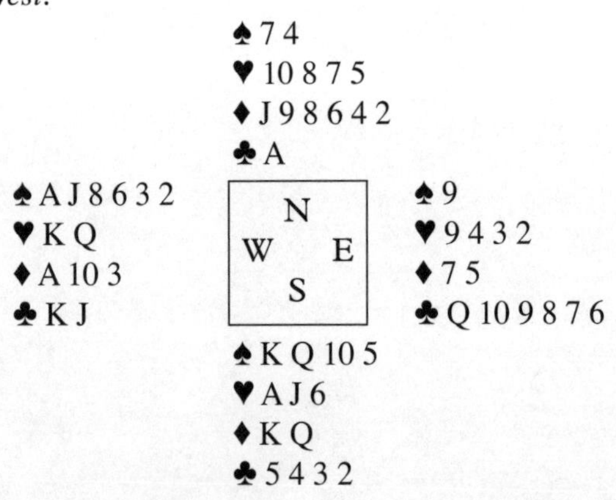

West	**North**	**East**	**South**
Baird			*Belladonna*
1 ♠	Pass	Pass	Dble
2 ♠	3 ♦	Pass	3 NT
All Pass			

West led ♠6, which ran to ♠4, ♠9 and ♠K. West assumed from this trick that her partner had ♠10. She lambasted herself for not doubling. It was, after all, a great chance to take a big penalty from a world champion.

Declarer led ♦K and West ducked. Declarer led ♦Q and West ducked again. Then came ♥J, taken by West's queen.

At this point West could see two potential entries to dummy, ♥10 and ♣A, but she anticipated that a small spade to partner's ten would clear Belladonna's queen, leaving four winners for when she got in with ♦A. But the lead of ♠2 was won by dummy's seven.

Declarer played ♥A to drop the king, then went across to ♥10 before leading a diamond. West won the ace but was now restricted to ♠A before leading into a winning spade or winning club. Declarer was then able to cash three diamonds.

Ten tricks.

Three No-trumps (plus one) from a combined twenty points and not much that defence could do about it.

WHEN TIME RAN OUT

OSLO, NORWAY, JULY 1969

France had started the 1969 European Ladies Championships as outsiders, but a string of good results took them to second place by the end of the penultimate round of matches. They were only one Victory Point behind leaders Great Britain, so the outcome would depend on the results of two matches in the final round – Britain against tenth-place Denmark and France against eleventh-place Greece.

In the latter match, the Victory Points were divided 6–2 in favour of Greece. Britain needed only two Victory Points to secure the Championships, and their match with Denmark was running neck and neck. But a drama was unfolding. Here's how the build-up was summarised by Count Bonde, president of the European Bridge League:

> The Tournament Director announced the start of play and the time when play should be concluded. According to the rules this is the only statement the Tournament Director is required to give the players regarding the time element. It is up to the players, assisted by their team's captain, if he is present, to keep track of the time.
>
> When one half-hour remained of the allotted time, the Tournament Director warned the players in the Great Britain–Denmark match that they were behind time and risking penalties of Victory Points. At a later stage the Tournament Director, a Norwegian, went up to their table and

> explained that the players had already forfeited two Victory Points and had a certain period of time before forfeiting three Victory Points. This caused some misunderstanding among the British players, who thought the Tournament Director was alluding to the time allotted to normal play. None of the players, nor the team captain, had apparently checked up on the time. The team captain, incidentally, told me later, that his watch was 'quite unreliable'. The match finished thirteen minutes late.

According to the tournament rules, teams received a warning on the first two occasions that they exceeded the time allotted for a match, but there were special rules on the last round of matches, when time faults were punished immediately. The penalty for being between six and ten minutes late was a loss of five IMPs from the total number of IMPs won during the Championships, a fairly minimal penalty. But the penalty for being more than ten minutes over time was two Victory Points, even though the offence may be the team's first of the tournament and had not been preceded by a warning.

So in this case, thirteen minutes over time, both teams should have been penalised two Victory Points.

This was how the match ended: Denmark 5 Great Britain 3.

This was how the score should have been adjusted: Denmark 3 Great Britain 1.

But this was how the score was actually submitted: Denmark 5 Great Britain 3.

Forms showing the starting and finishing times were usually handed in with the results, but this procedure was not followed after this crucial match, as Count Bonde explained in his later statement:

> Normally the penalty should have been brought to the knowledge of the 'results room'. By some mistake or omission this was not done. The Results Board thus announced the British team as winners of the Championships. When the omission to deduct the penalty points was brought to the notice of the Appeals Committee, this committee, after having heard everybody connected with the match, had no option but to

correct the score. Understandably, this came as a severe shock to the British Ladies' team, who for some hours had considered themselves champions.

With Great Britain losing 3–1 to Denmark and France being defeated 6–2 by Greece, the two contenders were now level on Victory Points, but France won on a better quotient (total IMPs won divided by total IMPs lost).

Strangely, when Great Britain had played France earlier, in the fourth round of matches, the British women had fought back to overcome a half-time deficit and win the match 73–49. This converted to 7–1 in Victory Points. Had the equality been decided by results against each other, the British would have won.

Count Bonde's statement had a sting in its final paragraph: 'The French Ladies' team now had achieved the best result, but very sportingly declined the Championship title. There was a noticeable lack of sportsmanship in some reactions to the decision of the Appeals Committee.'

Britain's final match, against Denmark, had been a tense affair. Here is a hand that must have needed some thought. It would have taken some people all night to play this one.

Dealer West. Game All.

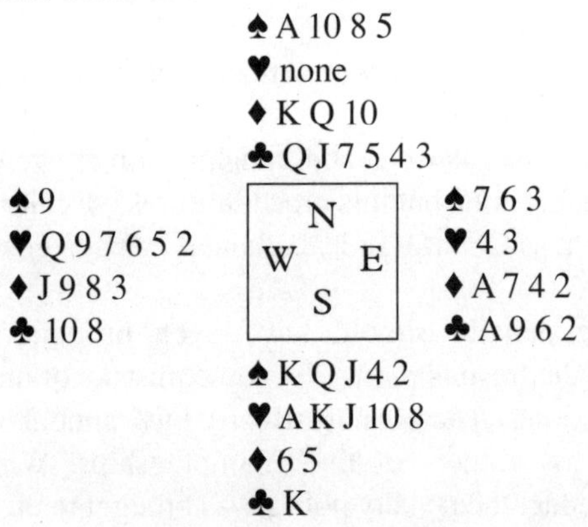

West	**North**	**East**	**South**
	Rixi Markus		*Fritzi Gordon*
Pass	1 ♣	Pass	2 ♠
Pass	3 ♠	Pass	4 ♦
Pass	4 ♥	Pass	4 ♠
Pass	5 ♦	Pass	6 ♠
All Pass			

The final contract of Six Spades was the same at both tables. The lead of ♥6 was also the same. This provided declarer with an immediate diamond discard. When Britain were North–South, Mrs Gordon drew trumps in three rounds and discarded two more diamonds on two top hearts. Next came ♣K, but the Danish East held up ♣A. That left declarer with only one entry to dummy, which was not enough to establish dummy's clubs. The contract went one off.

At the other table the British East, Jane Priday, also held up ♣A for the same result – one off.

No swing. Lots of sweat. The clock ticking away…

THE SHARIF BRIDGE CIRCUS

LONDON, 1970

The Sharif Bridge Circus was formed in 1967 to play exhibition matches against leading teams in Europe and North America. Movie star Omar Sharif took his team to big cities, where they played in front of Bridge-o-Rama audiences, television cameras, newspaper reporters, expert commentators and attractive groupies. The tours did a lot to popularise the game.

The 1970 tour ended with a 100-rubber challenge issued by the two British players, Jeremy Flint and Jonathan Cansino. The match was later reduced to 80 rubbers because of time pressures, but the stakes were £1 a point, plus an additional bonus of £1,000 on the net result of each four rubbers.

The match was played in the ballroom of the Piccadilly Hotel and one of the conditions was that Omar Sharif should play at least 60 rubbers. At the time he had huge drawing power, being that rare combination of international bridge player and celebrity actor. One time, when Sharif made a brilliant play at the bridge table, Terence Reese described it as the best thing Sharif had done since *Dr Zhivago*.

In his Bridge Circus, Sharif partnered either Claude Delmouly or Benito Garozzo, and the fourth member of the team was Giorgio Belladonna. This was probably the most discussed hand of the London match.

Dealer North. Game All.

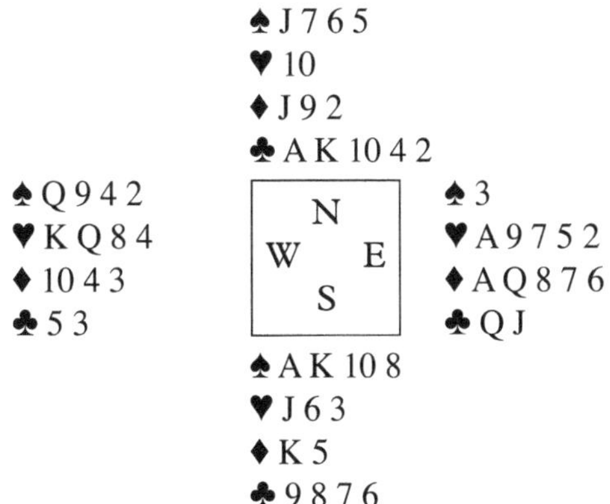

North: ♠J 7 6 5 ♥10 ♦J 9 2 ♣A K 10 4 2

West: ♠Q 9 4 2 ♥K Q 8 4 ♦10 4 3 ♣5 3

East: ♠3 ♥A 9 7 5 2 ♦A Q 8 7 6 ♣Q J

South: ♠A K 10 8 ♥J 6 3 ♦K 5 ♣9 8 7 6

West	**North**	**East**	**South**
Delmouly	*Cansino*	*Sharif*	*Flint*
	Pass	1 ♥	Pass
2 ♥	Dble	4 ♥	4 ♠
Dble	All Pass		

West led ♥K and Sharif played the nine. The Sharif team were playing the Blue Team Club, and Delmouly took ♦9 to mean strength in diamonds. He placed Sharif with ♥A and two top diamonds. He put declarer with ♣Q.

A second heart was ruffed low in dummy and a low spade went to the ten and queen. Delmouly switched to a diamond. Sharif won the ace and returned a diamond. South won and crossed to ♣A, Sharif playing the queen. Trumps were drawn and then everything depended on Jeremy Flint reading the clubs correctly. Flint finessed and lost the rest of the tricks. Had he played ♣K he would have won the remainder. A loss of 1,100 points rather than a gain of 790.

MINUS 3,500

LIVERPOOL, 1971

Declarer went twelve off on this rubber-bridge hand.

Dealer West. Game All (East–West 60).

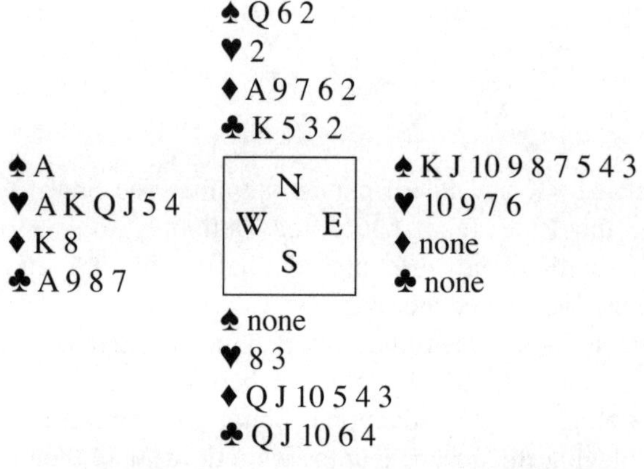

North: ♠ Q 6 2 ♥ 2 ♦ A 9 7 6 2 ♣ K 5 3 2

West: ♠ A ♥ A K Q J 5 4 ♦ K 8 ♣ A 9 8 7

East: ♠ K J 10 9 8 7 5 4 3 ♥ 10 9 7 6 ♦ none ♣ none

South: ♠ none ♥ 8 3 ♦ Q J 10 5 4 3 ♣ Q J 10 6 4

West	North	East	South
1 ♥	Pass	2 ♥	2 NT
4 ♥	5 ♣	5 ♥	Pass
6 ♥	Dble	Pass	6 ♠ (i)
Pass	Pass	7 ♥	Pass
Pass	7 ♠ (ii)	Dble	All Pass

(i) A cue bid to ask for a spade lead against Seven Hearts
(ii) Thinking partner is two-suited in spades and diamonds rather than the two minor suits

EGDIRB

ENGLAND, 1971

Egdirb may sound like a Swedish tennis player, or a two-year-old eating at the table, but it is actually bridge backwards. According to Hugh Darwen, in his definitive article in *Bridge Magazine* (May 1971), *egdirb* is ideal for those who are having a bad run of cards and need a change from normal bridge.

To play *egdirb rebbur* you start by shuffling the cards and placing them to the left. Your partner (*rentrap*) cuts the cards (away from the dealer) and then dealer deals anticlockwise (the direction that the *egdirb* bidding and play goes round the table). The honour cards are the twos, threes, fours and fives, and the twos are valued as four 'high-card' points. The highest card in the pack is ♣2, because the suit hierarchy is now clubs at the top (scoring 30 a trick), followed by diamonds (30), hearts (20) and spades (20). But no-trumps are still the highest of them all.

Tricks bid and made score above the line; penalties and bonuses go below. There are special penalties for bidding or playing out of turn, or for an illegal bid (like One Diamond over One Club) or for claiming a trick that you have not won. Darwen suggests 100 (non-vulnerable) and 200 (vulnerable), but that sounds steep.

In its most sophisticated form, *egdirb* involves saying technical bridge terms backwards.

'A warning – it is not as easy as it may sound,' said Darwen, but I am sure you have realised that already.

Here is an example. The participants made a delayed start after discussing a number of systems – the Blue Team Spade, basic

LOCA and Five-card Minors – and clarifying the rules.

'Does dealer bid first?'

'I think so.'

'That doesn't sound very abnormal.'

Yes, a few things are sacred – East is still East, and North is still North.

Dealer North. Love All.

	North	
	♣ 2 4 7 8 K	
	♦ 3 4 10 Q	
	♥ 7 9	
	♠ 7 9	
West		**East**
♣ 9		♣ 3 5 6 Q A
♦ 7 J		♦ 6 K
♥ 4 5 J Q K A		♥ 8 10
♠ 3 6 J K		♠ 4 10 Q A
	South	
	♣ 10 J	
	♦ 2 5 8 9 A	
	♥ 2 3 6	
	♠ 2 5 8	

West	**South**	**East**	**North**
			Ssap
Ssap	1 ♦	*Dibon*	3 ♦
Ssap	4 NT	*Dibon*	5 ♠
Ssap	5 ♦	*All Ssap*	

The bidding was slow and deliberate, with no penalties, although it took East and West a few minutes to come to terms with having bad hands. After South had opened his five-card minor and received a positive response, he used *Doowkcalb* to ask for twos. Unfortunately his *rentrap* overlooked her ♣2, which perhaps was not surprising as it was only the second *egdirb* bid of her life. South stopped short of the *mals llams* and was a little surprised when *ymmud* went down.

Declarer had a spade loser and a possible club loser. Indeed, East was confident of making a trick with ♣ 3 5 6 until it dawned on him that the finesse was going the other way round the table.

'Is the king still a king, or is it a *gnik*?' East asked, when he used ♦K to play low on the first diamond trick.

'I think it's still a king, but it's worth a lot less.'

'That's the first sensible thing you've said for a long time.'

Five Diamonds made with an overtrick.

North and South then spent five minutes debating their *mals* bidding, while East and West happily engaged in a discussion about whether they would bid Six Hearts or Six Spades if they were playing normal bridge. Everybody seemed happy.

A few days later, playing in a club, South looked at a freshly displayed dummy and said, 'Thank you, *rentrap* – ideal for *egdirb*.'

There were a few funny looks, but nobody called the *rotcerid*.

FOUR ACES OR NONE?

TAIPEI, TAIWAN, 1971

The oddest moment in the 1971 Bermuda Bowl came when a French player using the Blackwood Convention misinterpreted his partner's response of Five Clubs. Roger Trézel thought that Jean Louis Stoppa had four aces rather than none.

France, the European champions, did very well in these World Championships, eventually losing the final to the defending champions, the Dallas Aces. The misunderstanding occurred when France played Brazil in the last of the qualifying rounds.

Dealer East. Love All.

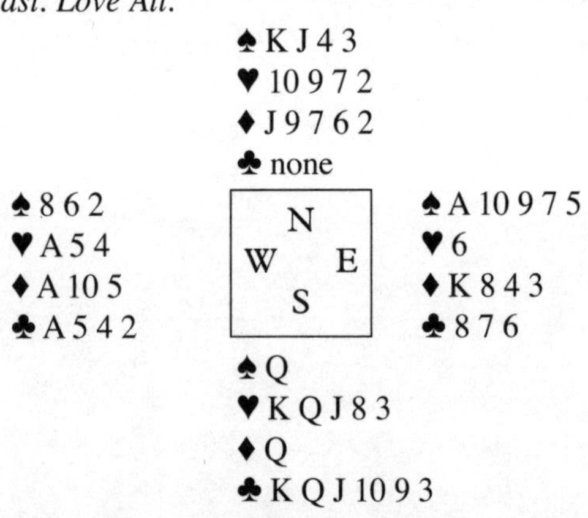

West	**North**	**East**	**South**
	Stoppa		*Trézel*
		Pass	1 ♣
Pass	1 ♦	Pass	1 ♥
Pass	3 ♥	Pass	4 NT
Pass	5 ♣	Pass	7 ♥
Dble	All Pass		

Trézel's bid of Four No-trumps required the traditional Blackwood response – Five Clubs (none or four), Five Diamonds (one), Five Hearts (two) or Five Spades (three). Trézel assumed that his partner had at least two aces to justify the jump to Three Hearts. He took Five Clubs to mean four aces and leaped to Seven Hearts.

'It might have been worse,' Trézel said later, after he had gone three down. 'East could have had the ace of clubs – or I might have redoubled.'

'To reach such a contract may seem ludicrous,' said Victor Mollo in *Bridge Magazine* (July 1971), 'but the "four aces or none" trap is one into which the best of us can fall from time to time.'

CARS FOR CARDS

NEW YORK CITY, MAY 1972

When Omar Sharif's Bridge Circus toured the United States in 1972, it was sponsored by the Lancia car manufacturing company. If Sharif's team could be beaten, the victors would win a fleet of six Lancia cars between them. Their first match, played over 60 boards in New York City, was in doubt until the final hand.

This was the 30th board of the match. It was played at midnight on the first evening and was described by one of the American players, Alan Sontag, as a 'rare and great hand'. In one room, Forquet and Sharif bid and made Six Diamonds. In the other room, Belladonna and Garozza represented the Sharif team.

Dealer West. Love All.

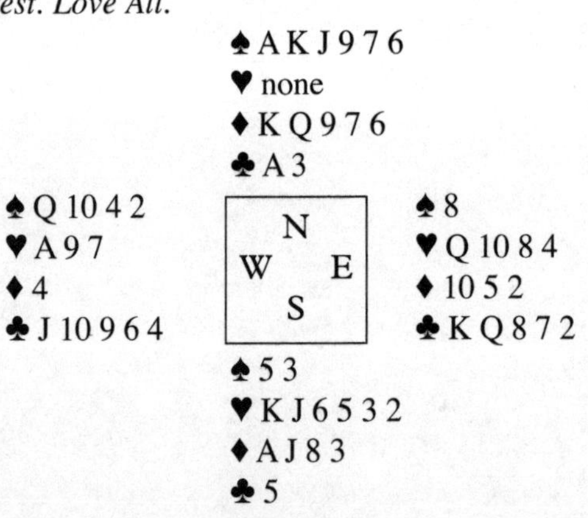

West	**North**	**East**	**South**
Belladonna	*Granovetter*	*Garozzo*	*Rubin*
Pass	1 ♣	2 ♣	2 ♥
4 ♣	Pass	Pass	4 ♦
Pass	5 NT	Pass	6 ♣
Pass	7 ♦	All Pass	

The odds favoured the grand slam to make, but the four–one split in spades rendered it almost impossible. Had the contract made, the Americans would have won eleven IMPs. Instead Sharif's team took fourteen IMPs to extend their first day's lead to 28 IMPs.

The Sharif lead was still 22 IMPs with only seven boards to play. Then the match swung in the Americans' favour, and the Americans sealed their victory by 25 IMPs on the last hand when Matt Granovetter made an optimistic contract of Six Clubs.

Omar Sharif conceded the match and Lancia provided the winners with cars. Sharif said later that he had become the number-one Lancia distributor in the United States.

A FLAT BOARD?

OSTEND, BELGIUM, 1973

When Ireland met Portugal in the 1973 European Championships, both rooms registered a score of 1,310 points.

'Flat board,' someone said.

Then they all looked more closely.

Dealer East. Love All.

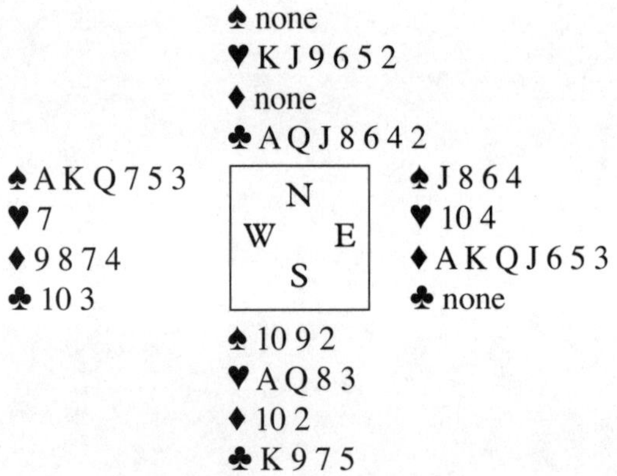

North: ♠ none ♥ K J 9 6 5 2 ♦ none ♣ A Q J 8 6 4 2

West: ♠ A K Q 7 5 3 ♥ 7 ♦ 9 8 7 4 ♣ 10 3

East: ♠ J 8 6 4 ♥ 10 4 ♦ A K Q J 6 5 3 ♣ none

South: ♠ 10 9 2 ♥ A Q 8 3 ♦ 10 2 ♣ K 9 7 5

Closed Room

West	**North**	**East**	**South**
	MacHale		*Pigot*
		1 ♦	Pass
1 ♠	Dble	2 ♠	3 ♥
4 ♠	6 ♥	Dble	All Pass

Open Room

West	**North**	**East**	**South**
O'Riordan		*Fitzgerald*	
		1 ♦	Pass
1 ♠	2 ♦	4 ♠	5 ♥
5 ♠	6 ♥	6 ♠	Dble
All Pass			

In the Closed Room, West (Portugal) failed to find the club lead, so South made all thirteen tricks to score 1,310 for Ireland.

In the Open Room, North (Portugal) failed to find the heart lead, so West made all thirteen tricks to score 1,310 for Ireland.

Not quite a flat board.

One Ireland player, Peter Pigot, was intrigued by the situation in the Open Room. He gave the North hand to a Danish friend and asked the friend to lead against Seven Spades.

'I always follow the golden rule in such situations,' Pigot's friend said. 'I lead my short suit, in this case hearts!'

Portugal finished 23rd out of 23 teams.

NORTH OR SOUTH?

ENGLAND, 1973

G C H Fox included this hand from a Life Masters Pairs tournament in his autobiography, *Grand Master of Bridge* (1999). Six No-trumps was a breeze when played by North (as was the case at some tables), but look what happened when South was the declarer in no-trumps.

Dealer East. North–South Game.

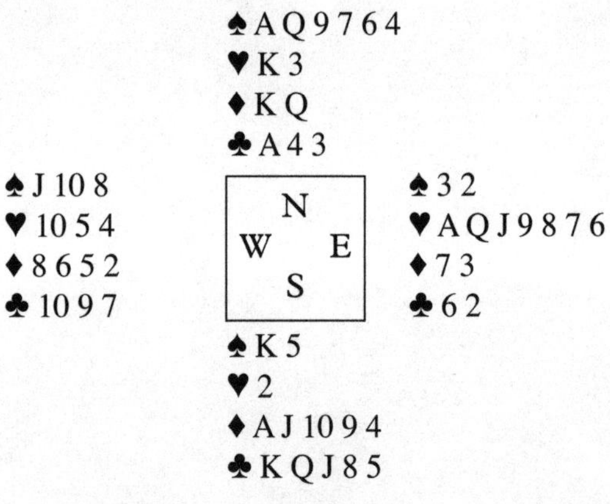

West	**North**	**East**	**South**
		3 ♥	3 NT (i)
Pass	6 NT (ii)	Pass	Pass
7 ♥	7 NT	Dble	All Pass

(i) Intended as the Unusual No-trump, showing minors
(ii) Misinterpreting partner's bid as natural with a heart stop

West led ♥10 and East took the first seven tricks to collect 2,000 points. Looking at the score from the East–West perspective, this compared very well with a successful Six No-trumps by North (minus 1,440) and Seven Spades made by another North (minus 2,210). In the latter case, East did not believe that hearts would go round.

THE BERMUDA INCIDENT

BERMUDA, 1975

Cheating allegations surfaced again at the 1975 Bermuda Bowl when officials of the North America team accused an Italian pair of communicating information by playing footsie under the table. Bridge administrators had already erected screens to conceal hand movements. Now they placed coffee tables below the tables to ensure that feet stayed in the appropriate quarter.

The confrontation had been simmering for some time. In *Popular Bridge* magazine, Alfred Sheinwold, the non-playing North America captain, had previously made allegations against an Italian pair, Gianfranco Facchini and Sergio Zucchelli. Now other players and officials said that they witnessed Facchini reaching out with his feet during auctions and before opening leads. Zucchelli kept his feet still so that Facchini could touch them with his own, it was said, but Facchini made no similar foot movements during the play of a hand. The implication was that signals were being passed between the two men, although there was no evidence of any coded communication and no correlation between specific foot movements and either the bidding or the play of the cards.

The World Bridge Federation heard evidence from the observers, including two non-American members of the World Bridge Federation executive council, who reported a total of eighteen foot-tapping incidents in 24 boards. Zucchelli testified that he was unaware of any foot movements by his partner. The WBF concluded that Facchini and Zucchelli 'be severely reprimanded for improper conduct with respect to the actions of Mr Facchini moving his feet unnaturally and touching his partner's feet during the auction and before the opening lead'.

The WBF had no proof that the pair were cheating, an outcome which divided participants almost entirely down national lines. Certain Americans were (and still are) convinced that Facchini and Zucchelli were cheating, while certain Europeans felt that the Americans were being unnecessarily paranoid or strategically persecutory. Facchini and Zucchelli were left out of the next two matches, but were brought back for the final between North America and Italy (see page 175).

Bridge Magazine, a British publication, summed up the incident as follows:

> Two points arise. The first is a well-known fact: that eye-witnesses, as every police force in the world will tell you, are unreliable, and when they are told in advance what to look for they are doubly unreliable. The second point is that players have mannerisms. They are not automatons. One of the best and most respected players in America taps his foot in moments of stress. Others cross and uncross their legs. Others again fiddle with their pencils. The Italian – and this is a matter of record; he was under observation for it in England last year – shuffles his feet about. Is this a cause for reprimand?

The chief accusers felt it would only have been a matter of time before proof against the Italians was discovered, and all that stopped the case going forward was that the suspicion was made public too soon.

'What the prosecution says is that Italian players were seen indulging in behaviour that can have no innocent explanation,' said Denis Howard in *Australian Bridge*. 'If you discover a stranger's hand on your wallet you conclude that he is attempting to steal your money. The legal maxim is *res ipsa loquitor*: the facts speak for themselves.'

Reading over the Bermuda Incident, some of the literature seems strangely emotive for such a seemingly technical, logical and intellectual game as bridge. The story itself was sadly confusing, partly because the bridge authorities had no clear impartial guidelines on how to investigate suspected cheats. For instance, the stopgap match monitor at the centre of the initial observations was a *Philadelphia Inquirer* reporter who had been previously briefed on the possibility of the Italian pair cheating. The reporter then took his own observations to an American player rather than an appropriate official. The reporter was dismissed as a story chaser by the defence, while the prosecution argued that he had overcome his initial scepticism by collecting convincing evidence.

One clear outcome was the need for bridge players to be seen to be not cheating; or rather, not to be seen to be not cheating. A structure of screens and curtains was introduced for the next Bermuda Bowl.

As Henry Francis and Brian Senior said in *The Bermuda Bowl* (1999):

> In Monte Carlo [in 1976] the screens bisected the table right to the floor. In fact, the tables were specially constructed to allow the plywood to go through the centre both up and down. In addition, the screens hung vertically. After the auction was completed, a monitor and an observer lifted the loose part of the curtain a few inches and attached it to hooks provided for that purpose. This left a space of about five inches – enough to see the cards played on the other side of the table but not enough to see partner's face, just his hands.

Students of strange hands waited for the next development. Sure enough, in the 1977 Bermuda Bowl an American player, Ira Rubin, misheard the monitor's spoken relay of the bids on the other side of the screen. A bizarre auction saw Rubin supporting diamonds three times before he realised that the opposition had bid diamonds rather than his partner.

HAND OF THE CENTURY?

BERMUDA, 1975

The final of the 1975 Bermuda Bowl, played in Bermuda to celebrate 25 years of the competition, was referred to by one contemporary publication as 'the most exciting and bitter struggle in the history of the event'.

The 96-board final between North America and Italy was played against the background of the cheating allegations levelled at Facchini and Zucchelli. The North American team deplored the failure of the World Bridge Federation to bar the accused Italians from the competition. Then, on the morning of the first session of the final, the Americans were outraged to discover that Facchini and Zucchelli were in Italy's starting line-up. Alfred Sheinwold, North America's non-playing captain, announced that his team would not play against this pair unless instructed to do so by the American Contract Bridge League. The ACBL representatives in Bermuda unanimously ordered the team to play.

Italy started the final very badly. Facchini and Zucchelli were playing with frayed nerves and there was undoubtedly tension around the match. At the halfway stage, after 48 boards, the North Americans led by 138 IMPs to 65.

In the second half, with Facchini and Zucchelli left out at the request of Benito Garozzo and Giorgio Belladonna, the Italians rallied brilliantly. When it came to the last few boards, Italy led by thirteen IMPs. This hand (Board 92 of the 96) decided the match.

Dealer West. East–West Game.

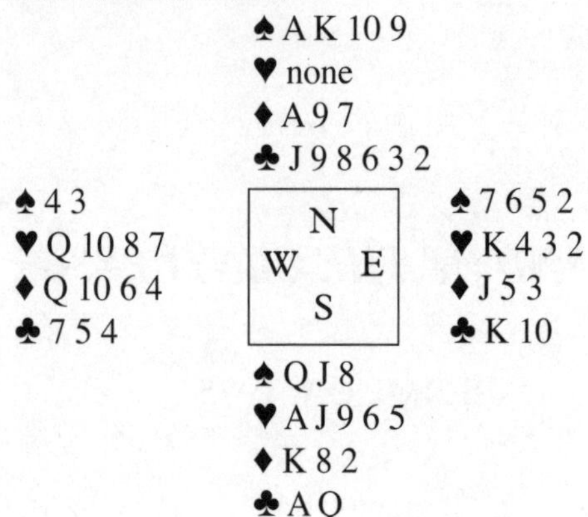

Closed Room

West	**North**	**East**	**South**
Franco	*Hamman*	*Pittala*	*Wolff*
Pass	1 ♠	Pass	2 ♥
Pass	3 ♣	Pass	4 NT
Pass	5 ♥	Pass	6 NT
All Pass			

Open Room

West	**North**	**East**	**South**
Eisenberg	*Belladonna*	*Kantar*	*Garozzo*
Pass	2 ♣	Pass	2 ♦
Pass	2 ♠	Pass	3 ♥
Pass	3 NT	Pass	4 ♣
Pass	4 ♦	Pass	4 NT
Pass	5 ♦	Pass	5 ♥
Dble	Redble	Pass	5 ♠
Pass	5 NT	Pass	7 ♣
All Pass			

Spectators observing the Vu-graph were aware of events in the Closed Room, where the Americans had made thirteen tricks in Six No-trumps. Could the Italians emulate them in the Open Room?

It took Garozzo and Belladonna fourteen bids before they reached a contract of Seven Clubs. The chances seemed slim, but

Belladonna finessed ♣K and then dropped it under the ace. The 29-point grand slam brought a decisive twelve-IMP swing on the hand and Italy went on to win the final 215–189. Had the Italians' contract gone off by one trick, the Americans would have won the final by three IMPs.

At the presentation dinner, warfare nearly broke out between the two sets of rival supporters.

'DIRECTOR'

DJERBA, TUNISIA, 1980

This hand was dealt at the 1980 Festival of Djerba.

Dealer West.

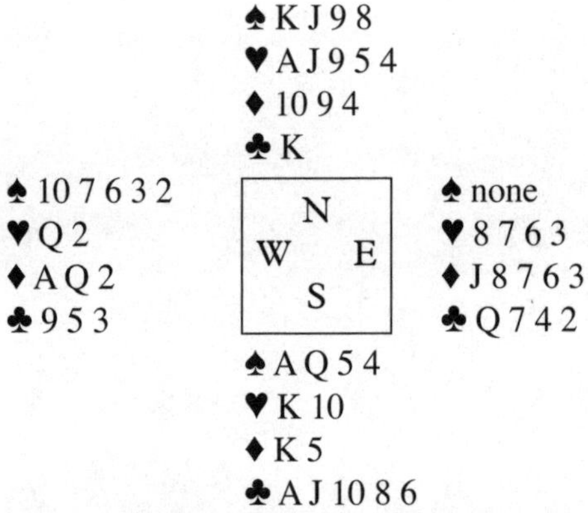

Most North–South pairs bid to Six Spades, the outcome of which depended on the lead. At one table, when Six Spades was doubled by West, North hesitated before passing. West immediately called the director.

In his book of famous hands *Bridge* (1990), José Le Dentu recalls how West outlined his case to the director: 'I doubled Six Spades and this man [politely indicating his left-hand opponent] hesitated before passing. He may have been thinking of transferring to Six No-trumps. In any case, I claim that South must pass.'

While the director considered this protest, South said that he was happy to pass. The hand was played in Six Spades (doubled). West led ♦A, followed by a small spade. Declarer took one spade, two hearts, ♦K and two clubs before ruffing a diamond and a club. The last four tricks were made with a high cross-ruff.

Six Spades made and yet Six No-trumps was highly likely to go down, except when West led a small diamond (as happened at one table).

Was the protest reasonable? Was justice done?

STRANGE BIDDING SYSTEMS

BIRMINGHAM, JULY 1981

One of the strangest components of bridge, as viewed by outsiders, is the requirement that players explain their bids. In most sports and games, officials and players try to keep their strategy secret. One cannot imagine a soccer coach filling in a convention card informing opponents of set-play options practised in training.

Some bridge players frown on the need to explain their actions. I have seen excellent flair players struggle to explain a bid to opponents, and some high-class players can make a mockery of the question-and-answer requirement.

'What does that lead mean?'

'Well, he started with thirteen cards and now he's got twelve.'

Mumblings and grumblings about inexplicable systems have been around for a long time. They probably reached their peak in the mid-1980s, when the Forcing Pass system was banned by bridge authorities.

Iceland caused an outcry by arriving at the 1952 European Championships armed with the groundbreaking Marmic system. Named after *Mar*io Franco and *Mic*hele Giovine, the Marmic system was described by *The Bridge Players' Encyclopedia* (1967) as 'probably the most unusual system ever played in serious international competition by a major bridge country'. Its most surprising feature was a *pass* in first or second position with a balanced hand and between sixteen and nineteen points. Conversely, an opening bid of One Club could mean a very strong hand, a normal club opener or a very weak hand.

A number of highly developed Forcing Pass or Variable Forcing Pass systems followed. A Polish system in the mid-1970s required a pass on seventeen points in first or second position, and at the 1984 Seattle World Team Olympiad a Danish pair used the Swedish Simple Super Spade system, whereby a pass in first or second seat showed any hand with eight or more points and four or more spades. The Danes had not supplied sufficient supplementary sheets to accompany their convention card, so their Italian opponents received permission to keep a copy of 'defence to the Super Spade' at hand during the first sixteen boards of the match. A confusion about whether this ruling applied to later boards in the match led to one of the Italian players withdrawing in protest.

In Britain, the Sowter-Lodge system made it to the 1981 European Championships, where Great Britain finished second and qualified for the Bermuda Bowl. The Sowter-Lodge pass, when vulnerable in first or second seat, showed either between zero and six points or seventeen-plus points. Their One Club bid meant between seven and ten points.

Also in that Great Britain team were John Collings and Paul Hackett, who deserved an entertainment award for their play in Birmingham. Collings and Hackett passed any hand of between nine and twelve points, and their One Club opener meant between zero and eight points, a normal club opener or a balanced hand with between twenty and 23 points. Collings played one vulnerable hand in One Diamond on a two-two fit and lost only 300 points. He made Six Diamonds off 22 high-card points, deliberately dropping a singleton king in an outside suit which split three-one, and on another hand found himself in Six Clubs with a total of five trumps.

'John Collings caught the eye many times with fine play,' wrote Terence Reese, reviewing the 1981 European Championships. 'He is the sort of player who discomposes opponents. Paul Hackett did well, often deceiving the opponents by the confident way in which he played difficult hands.'

Here is Board 13 of the Poland vs. Great Britain match.

Dealer South. Game All.

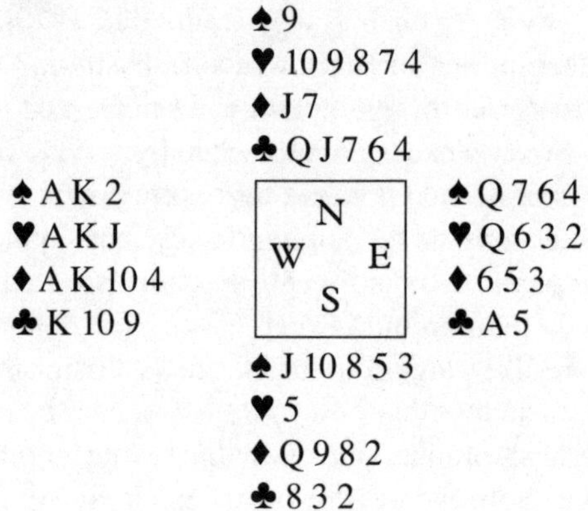

West	North	East	South
	Collings		*Hackett*
			1 ♣
Pass	1 ♦	Pass	Pass
Dble	1 ♥	Dble	1 ♠
Dble	2 ♣	Dble	All Pass

Poland had to defend brilliantly to put the contract five off and make 1,400 points, while in the other room Irving Rose and Robert Sheehan scored 1,440 points for Great Britain by making Six No-trumps.

I am not sure this board counted as a success – except by standards of strangeness – but the Collings–Hackett system did very well in those Championships as a whole. It was less successful in the Bermuda Bowl, where Great Britain narrowly failed to progress to the semi-finals.

In 1985 Forcing Pass systems were banned by the authorities on the grounds that they were too dominant. Opponents could not play their systems without opening first in hand or devising a complicated defence system, often at short notice. The furore split opinion about bridge authorities. The establishment believed that the bridge world could do without such complex, weird, dominating ideas from people bred in bidding laboratories. Others said that bidding was a critical part of the game and people should be allowed to develop systems at all levels as alternatives to 'Granny Acol'.

The Variable Forcing Pass system was seen by its exponents as one of the most foolproof bridge systems ever invented. It is still possible to find a complex set of notes that covers every conceivable option. Four of us once had an experimental evening at home with a simpler form of the Forcing Pass.

'Apparently you can't use the Forcing Pass in bridge clubs,' said one player. 'Only in the Bermuda Bowl.'

'It must be more like playing in the Bermuda Triangle,' another replied.

'Pass,' said dealer, smiling.

'What can I say?' said the next player. 'I can't double a pass.'

Our debate had begun.

ON LEAD IN THE BERMUDA BOWL FINAL

PORT CHESTER, NEW YORK, 1981

This was Board 72 of the 96-board Bermuda Bowl final between Pakistan and North America. The latter led by 68 IMPs before this hand. A time for caution?

Dealer West. Love All.

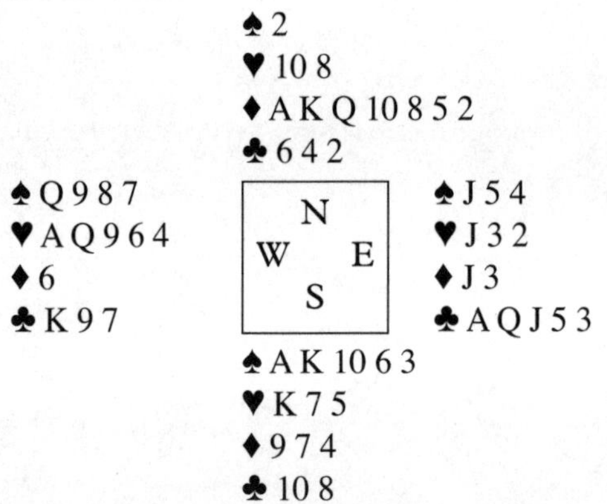

Open Room

West	**North**	**East**	**South**
Solodar	*Masood*	*Levin*	*Zia*
2 ♦ (i)	Pass	2 ♥	Pass
Pass	3 ♦	3 ♥	Pass
Pass	4 ♦	All Pass	

(i) Four spades, five hearts, twelve–seventeen high-card points

Closed Room

West	**North**	**East**	**South**
Munir	*Meckstroth*	*Fazli*	*Rodwell*
1 ♥	3 ♥ (i)	Dble	3 NT
Pass	Pass	Dble	Pass
Pass	Redble (ii)	All Pass	

(i) Asking his partner to bid 3 NT if he can stop hearts
(ii) SOS, showing doubt about No-trumps

Pakistan's North–South pair made Four Diamonds in the Open Room, but the North American 'Meckwell' partnership bid to a much riskier contract of Three No-trumps (redoubled) in the Closed Room. Much depended on Munir's opening lead. A club lead could give Pakistan the first ten tricks for 2,200 points and twenty IMPs.

Munir calculated that his partner had a black ace but guessed wrongly. He led a spade and Rodwell made his contract for 750 points. Instead of twenty IMPs to Pakistan it was twelve IMPs to North America. North America went on to win the final by 271 points to 182.33.

AN OBVIOUS SACRIFICE

HUBERT PHILLIPS TROPHY, JUNE 1983

Richard Fleet drew attention to this unusual hand in a letter published in *Bridge Plus* (June 2000).

Dealer West. East–West Game.

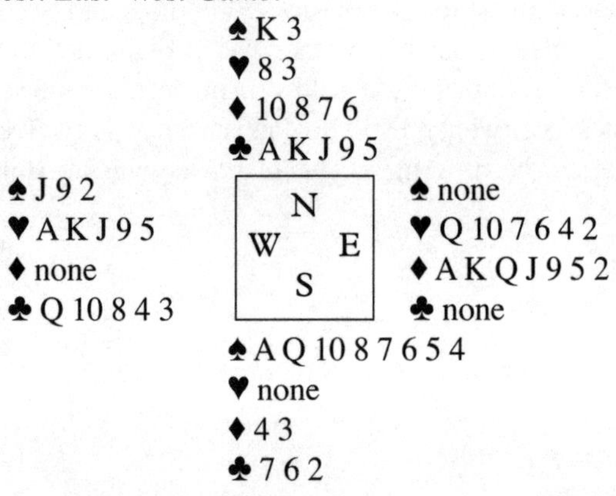

West	**North**	**East**	**South**
	Fleet		*Bailey*
1 ♥	2 ♣	5 NT	6 ♠
7 ♥	7 ♠	Dble	All Pass

Fleet (North) recalls the start of the hand: 'A low heart (a good shot) was led and I tabled the dummy and went to the bar, where I was asked how the match was going. I said that there had been nothing exciting and added, as an afterthought, that Phil [Bailey] was playing a doubled grand, but it was an obvious sacrifice.'

West's low heart, to East's queen, was presumably led in hope of a diamond ruff. Declarer trumped the heart and then, after a long think, led ♣2 to dummy's five. A very deep finesse. The five held the trick.

Declarer removed opponents' trumps and then took a second club finesse. He trumped a heart, finessed clubs for the third time and made Seven Spades (doubled) – *an obvious sacrifice.*

As Fleet points out, had West covered the low club with the eight, then it is much trickier. The correct play was to lead the six or seven from hand and let that run.

It certainly stopped the opposition making Seven Hearts, but there was no swing. The other room had exactly the same result.

A KIDNAPPING AND A CLOSE FINISH

WASHINGTON DC, JULY 1984

The 1984 American Contract Bridge League Summer Nationals Tournament was probably the strangest bridge event of all time: one team withdrew after accusations of impropriety; a bridge player kidnapped another bridge player and while the victim's husband was absent organising the ransom money, his team reached the Spingold Trophy final; and then the Spingold final was settled by an administrative mix-up that led to one board being redealt some hours after the match seemed over.

In the early part of the ten-day congress, the main talking point among the 4,000 competitors was the possibility of cheating, but that was replaced by the kidnapping of 60-year-old Edith Rosenkranz, who had helped her team to a second-place finish in the Masters Mixed Pairs. On the Thursday night, at 11.50 p.m., Mrs Rosenkranz was seeing a friend to a car on the fourth level of the Sheraton-Washington Hotel car park when a man abducted her at gunpoint. She was blindfolded and driven to a hideout.

Nearly 100 FBI agents were assigned to the case and armed police officers became a familiar sight in the tournament hotel. At one point a group of FBI officers was seen running at top speed along a hotel corridor. A series of phone calls to the victim's husband, George Rosenkranz, culminated in a large ransom demand, rumoured to be in excess of $1 million. Rosenkranz was a wealthy man. He had been president of the Syntex Pharmaceutical Company for 30 years before retiring two years earlier.

George Rosenkranz was also at the forefront of competitive bridge. He was playing captain of the third favourites to take the 1984 Spingold Trophy. The rules stipulated that all six players had to play a certain number of hands, but that rule was waived to allow Rosenkranz to deal with the more pressing business of delivering the ransom money.

He followed instructions by driving to a hospital in Alexandria, Virginia, and leaving the money in a car park. It was collected by two men in a van, which was kept under surveillance by FBI agents. Two hours later, the kidnappers were apprehended at the corner of Fifteenth Avenue and Constitution Avenue, and Edith Rosenkranz was released. A key to a Holiday Inn room found on one of the two men led the FBI agents to a third man, who was also arrested. One of the accused was a 42-year-old Life Master who had played with the Rosenkranz team early in his career. He had been missing from the bridge scene for the previous two years but had appeared that week in the Summer Nationals. Seven months later he was sentenced to three consecutive life terms in federal prison for having masterminded the kidnapping.

When tournament officials announced that Mrs Rosenkranz was 'alive and well and unharmed' after 46 hours in captivity, a big cheer went through the congress and spontaneous applause burst out. But it was not the first bridge-napping incident. In 1977 Mauritius Caransa, a wealthy Dutch businessman, was kidnapped outside his bridge club in Amsterdam. Caransa negotiated his own release for a ransom payment of £2.5 million.

Meanwhile, back at the 1984 Summer Nationals, the Rosenkranz team continued its progress to the Spingold Trophy final, relying on four players – Larry Cohen, Marty Bergen, Jeff Meckstroth and Eric Rodwell – rather than six. The Rosenkranz team led comfortably for much of the final, but a late rally from their opponents, captained by Alan Sontag, brought a nailbiting totting up of the scores. At first it looked as though Sontag's team had won by one IMP. Then it looked as though Rosenkranz's team had won by four IMPs. And then came the additional twist. It transpired that one deal had been 'misduplicated by officials' because the North and East hands had been interchanged in one room. The ruling was that an extra deal should replace this one board.

The Rosenkranz team had lost fifteen IMPs on this particular board, so that left the Sontag team seeking a twenty-IMP swing on the replacement board. At about 3.30 a.m., after a break of several hours, the two teams sat down to face this one-off deal.

Dealer South. Game All.

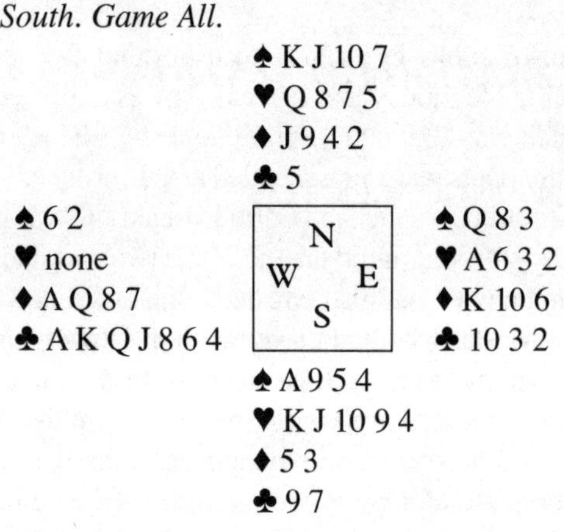

West	**North**	**East**	**South**
	Sion		*Sontag*
			4 ♥
5 ♣	6 ♥	Dble	Redble
All Pass			

West	**North**	**East**	**South**
			Pass
7 ♣	All Pass		

Sontag's team bid courageously, but Six Hearts (redoubled) went four down on the lead of ♣K, and Seven Clubs in the other room was two off on a spade lead. The hand did bring a big swing, but the wrong way for Alan Sontag, so George Rosenkranz ended an eventful week with the Spingold Trophy.

WATERLOO STATION

LONDON, OCTOBER 1985

Waterloo Station, one of London's busiest venues, offers a snapshot of the city. If you hang around long enough, overhearing and observing, smelling and tasting coffee, you can form opinions about contemporary life – style and fashion, language and communication, tourism and cosmopolitanism. You can see a range of activities – a poetry reading, a business meeting, a job interview – while hearing one end of innumerable mobile-phone conversations and not hearing Tannoy announcements. No wonder Waterloo Station was chosen as the subject for the 'fly-on-the-wall' documentary called *Terminus* that launched the career of film director John Schlesinger.

Naturally, bridge has been played at Waterloo. In October 1985 two top British players, Jeremy Flint and Victor Mollo, set up a table on the station and challenged travellers to play specially prepared hands.

It is less common to play on station concourses than it is to play on trains. Commuter bridge has been popular at times in Britain and the United States, but these days it must be hard to find regular partners and even harder to commandeer four seats together. Commuters can play on a daily basis or over a longer period. Americans use the term 'tunnel bid' to describe a wild bid intended to make up lost points as the train approaches one of the New York stations.

I have often thought about walking up and down the aisle of a train, saying, 'Would anyone like a game of bridge?' Indeed, after a three-hour delay was announced one day, I even wondered if there were enough players for a waiting-room duplicate competition.

Jeremy Flint and Victor Mollo had no trouble attracting opponents when they set up their table on Waterloo Station, and Flint later wrote up the story of one hand for *The Times*. The challengers succeeded well enough on this particular hand to win the 'latest sophisticated bridge computer'.

To test commuters, Flint and Mollo chose a specimen hand that called for the execution of Morton's Fork Coup, also known as the Dilemma Coup. Cardinal John Morton, chancellor to King Henry VII, was a zealous collector of taxes. He believed that rich people who lived lavishly could afford to pay taxes, while poor people who lived modestly must have plenty of savings to pay their taxes. There was no answer to Morton – he got you on his fork either way.

Here was a chance for South to do the same while playing Six Spades.

Dealer West. Love All.

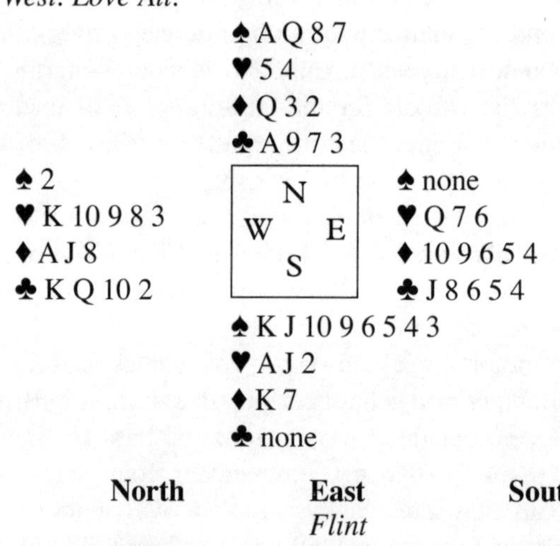

West	**North**	**East**	**South**
Mollo		*Flint*	
1 ♥	Dble	Pass	6 ♠
All Pass			

West led ♣K and a quick strategy check showed two possible losers, ♦A and a heart. Given a kindly lead – a heart would have caused insurmountable problems – South ruffed in hand, drew trumps in one round with ♠K and then led a small diamond. If East has ♦A then this is no help, but in fact West held the ace. If West plays the ace then declarer can discard two hearts on ♣A and ♦Q. If West ducks, as he did, declarer can go up with ♦Q and then throw away the losing diamond on ♣A, conceding a heart at the end.

This was a clear example of Morton's Fork Coup, but the oddity came from where it was played. Waterloo Station thus joined a list of strange bridge venues, which includes supermarkets, coaches and, as already mentioned (see page 74), battlefields. In September 1999 *The Times* carried a story about two Taiwanese brothers who had played bridge while trapped in earthquake rubble for five days in Taipei. The brothers survived on a few apples, some water and, when everything ran out, by drinking their own urine. But another report, in the *Guardian*, suggested that the brothers were playing poker rather than bridge, which is more likely given there were only two of them.

A better example of 'bridge while awaiting rescue' was that experienced by an American soldier in the late 1960s: 'After the Vietcong bomb had exploded, trapping the four of us in the bar, there was nothing we could do until a rescue team arrived. I found a pack of cards and we settled down to a friendly game of bridge.'

Yes, it takes a war to make bridge friendly.

SAME CONTRACT, VERY DIFFERENT RESULT

SÃO PAULO, BRAZIL, 1985

When Chinese Taipei met Argentina in the 1985 Venice Cup, both teams happened upon the same contract on Board 25, but events in the two rooms had little else in common.

Dealer East. Love All.

	North	
	♠ J 10 ♥ 10 9 8 7 5 4 ♦ A J 8 7 3 ♣ none	
West ♠ 9 7 ♥ J ♦ Q 4 ♣ K Q 9 8 7 4 3 2	N W E S	**East** ♠ 4 3 2 ♥ K Q 6 3 ♦ 9 6 2 ♣ J 6 5
	♠ A K Q 8 6 5 ♥ A 2 ♦ K 10 5 ♣ A 10	

Room 1

West	**North**	**East**	**South**
Argentina	*Chinese Taipei*	*Argentina*	*Chinese Taipei*
		Pass	1 ♣ (i)
5 ♣	5 ♥	Pass	5 ♠
Pass	6 ♦	Pass	7 NT
All Pass			

(i) Precision club (sixteen high-card points or more)

Room 2

West	**North**	**East**	**South**
Chinese Taipei	*Argentina*	*Chinese Taipei*	*Argentina*
		Pass	2 ♣
5 ♣	5 ♥	Pass	6 ♣
Pass	6 ♦	Pass	7 ♣
Pass	Pass	Dble	7 NT
Pass	Pass	Dble	All Pass

In Room 1, declarer won the opening lead (♣K) and crossed to dummy to take ♠J and ♠10. She played a heart to her ace and ran her four winning spades (throwing hearts). Next came ♦K and then a small diamond. The queen dropped and it was a simple matter to go across to dummy's winning diamonds and make thirteen tricks for 1,520 points.

In Room 2, a mix-up over cue bids in clubs put North–South on track for a diabolical contract of Seven Clubs. They were rescued by East's double, much to the chagrin of West, who might have been wondering what seven down meant in IMPs. In fact, the Chinese made a better result from Seven No-trumps (doubled). Declarer guessed ♦Q was with East and had to take the finesse early. She won the club lead, played a diamond to dummy's ace and then another diamond to her ten. North won ♦Q and cashed seven clubs to put the contract eight down. Chinese Taipei had won another 1,500 points (on the scoring of the day) and 22 IMPs on the hand. If ♦Q had been with East, Argentina would have won nineteen IMPs instead.

As Nikos Sarantakos wrote in *Bridge Plus* (June 2000):

> This deal indeed sets many records. Not only has it the lowest point count for a Seven No-trump contract, it also probably holds the record for the largest difference in the number of tricks made at two tables in the same contract (eight), the biggest relative swing arising from a single action (41 IMPs), the highest number of undertricks in a freely bid slam (eight), and the biggest swing in a World Championship match (22 IMPs or 3,020 points).

TRICKS IN BATCHES

IRELAND, MAY 1987

A variation of the complete misfit comes when one pair stumbles into a No-trump contract. Tricks then come in batches, and who gets them often depends on the opening lead. Or maybe a few other things, like on this deal.

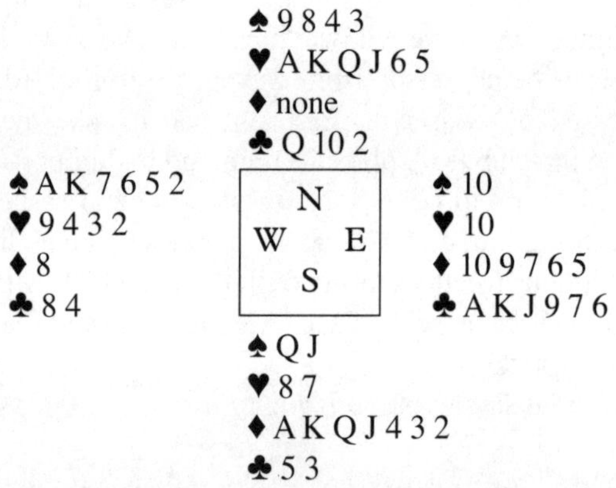

South played the hand in Three No-trumps. I have no record of the bidding and could not even try to guess it.

West led a small spade, which ran to the jack. South's eyes now lit up at the thought of cashing seven diamonds and six hearts for a total of fourteen tricks (if fourteen were needed).

What an excellent gambling Three No-trumps, South thought, playing ♦A and discarding a spade. *Could we have bid a slam?* He played ♦K and discarded a club. *It doesn't matter what I discard as long as it's not a heart*, he thought, cashing the ♦Q and ♦J, and throwing two more spades. *Five tricks. Eight more to go. Nearly time to claim the rest.*

South played ♦4 and was shocked when it lost to East's ten. He had not noticed West's discard on the second diamond. Now it was East's turn to collect a clump of tricks. He cashed six clubs before returning a spade to his partner's ace.

Declarer's vision of 'four over' had turned into 'four off'. Had he noticed West's discard on the second diamond, he could have gone across to the hearts after the fourth diamond and collected a batch of six heart tricks, making eleven tricks in total.

Had West led a club, or led ♠A for a look-see and then switched to a club, declarer would not have had much chance to daydream.

A MAMMOTH PENALTY

OCHO RIOS, JAMAICA, 1987

We have seen how penalties can run to thousands of points in rubber bridge (e.g. pages 110 and 124), but the world's best players can also get into trouble. Here is an example from when Great Britain played Sweden in the 1987 Bermuda Bowl. The British bid and made Three Diamonds on the East–West cards in the Closed Room. Meanwhile, in the Open Room…

Dealer East. Game All.

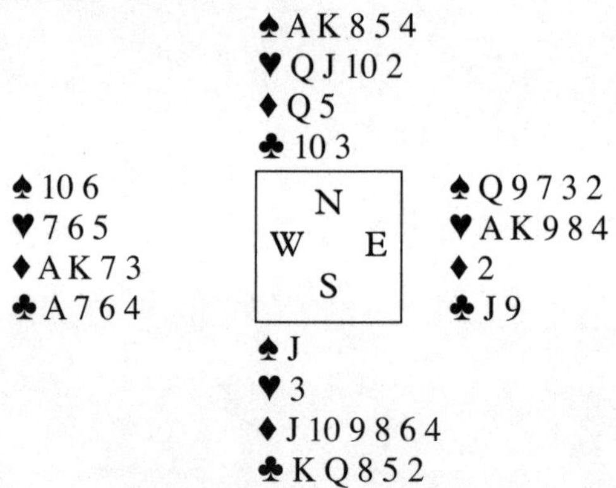

West	**North**	**East**	**South**
Forrester	*Lindkvist*	*Armstrong*	*Fallenius*
		2 NT (i)	Pass
3 ♥ (ii)	Pass	Pass	3 NT (iii)
Dble	Pass	Pass	Redble (iv)
All Pass			

(i) Seven–ten high-card points and at least five–five in two suits other than clubs
(ii) Pass or correct to Four Diamonds
(iii) Two-suited in the minors
(iv) SOS

Tony Forrester (West) led ♥5 for the British defenders. Declarer played dummy's ♥10 and lost to the king. John Armstrong (East) returned ♥9, which declarer ducked. East then led ♣9. Declarer played ♣K and West ducked. Declarer led ♠J to ♠A and then a heart from dummy. East won the heart and returned ♣J to ♣Q and West's ace. West cashed two top diamonds and then led ♠10. East overtook and led a heart to dummy. Declarer's last trick was ♠K, while defence still had two to take.

Five down (redoubled and vulnerable) for minus 2,800 points.

28 POINTS AND YET…

VENICE, ITALY, 1988

Any hand with 28 high-card points must be considered strange. When partner contributes a further five points, the hand becomes even more exciting. But, as we have seen before, high-card points don't mean everything.

This hand was documented by Terence Reese and David Bird in their book *Famous Hands from Famous Matches* (1991). Here is what happened when Canada played New Zealand in the 1988 World Olympiad.

Dealer West. North–South Game.

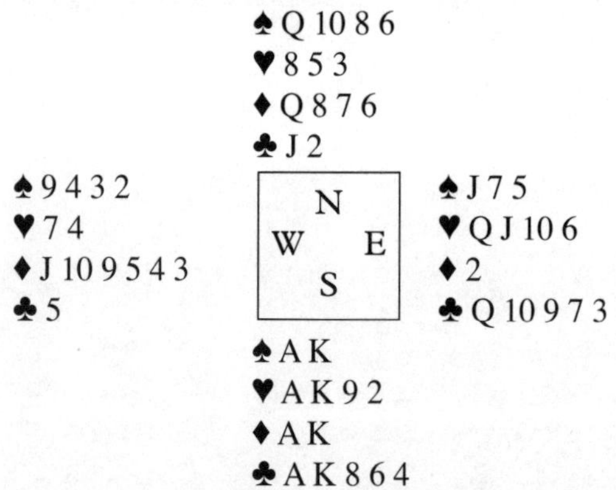

West		North / South		East
		♠ Q 10 8 6 ♥ 8 5 3 ♦ Q 8 7 6 ♣ J 2		
♠ 9 4 3 2 ♥ 7 4 ♦ J 10 9 5 4 3 ♣ 5		N W E S		♠ J 7 5 ♥ Q J 10 6 ♦ 2 ♣ Q 10 9 7 3
		♠ A K ♥ A K 9 2 ♦ A K ♣ A K 8 6 4		

Room 1

West	**North**	**East**	**South**
New Zealand	*Canada*	*New Zealand*	*Canada*
1 ♠ (i)	Pass	3 ♣	Dble
Pass	3 ♠	Pass	3 NT
All Pass			

(i) Zero–eight points or a balanced nine points

Room 2

West	**North**	**East**	**South**
Canada	*New Zealand*	*Canada*	*New Zealand*
3 ♦	Pass	3 ♥	6 NT
All Pass			

In Room 1, West led a club and South scrambled nine tricks.

In Room 2, West led a heart to the ten and ace. Declarer then took two top spades and two top diamonds in hand, and led a club to the jack and queen. East led ♠J, whereas a lead from the other suits would have doomed the contract. Instead, declarer took the two spades on the table (to make seven tricks), ♦Q and then somehow squeezed East into conceding the last four, making Six No-trumps.

Well, what do you expect with 33 points?

THE BRITOIL CASE

ABERDEEN, SCOTLAND, JUNE 1988

I remember visiting friends near Aberdeen in the late 1980s. Their young children had gone to bed and we were sitting around a log fire when I casually mentioned that I was playing more and more bridge.

My friends looked at each other and grinned.

'We know about you bridge players,' one of them told me. 'The trouble you get into.'

I must have looked puzzled.

'The Britoil case?' he prompted.

'Huh?'

So they told me about the Britoil case, and afterwards we had a game of Scrabble.

In June 1988, Alison Anders was a 30-year-old secretary working in the Britoil office in Aberdeen. She was an archaeology graduate whose interests were climbing, compiling quizzes, rowing and playing bridge. She was a member of the Westburn Bridge Club, where she partnered a work colleague called Royston Allen.

One night at the bridge club Anders chatted to a friend about her work. She mentioned in passing that it was possible for someone to take funds from the Britoil company. It was not worth bothering with petty amounts, Anders hinted, better to make it really worthwhile. Her friend thought little more of their conversation. After all, it wasn't unusual for people to remove jotters and pens from the workplace and talk about getting rich quick.

The bridge club provided Alison Anders and Roy Allen with opportunities to meet away from Roy Allen's wife. On club nights they discussed Britoil and developed their affair at Anders's flat in Aberdeen. Their plan involved a £23 million payment for the lease of a North Sea oil-drilling rig. The payment would come into a Britoil bank account and Anders could raise the paperwork to divert the funds. Some Middle East contacts of Roy Allen arranged to set up a Swiss bank account that could receive the cash. When the money reached there, it would be withdrawn with the sanction of a bank official and collected in a garbage vehicle.

The plan was put into effect on 23 June. But a Glasgow bank official, worried by an instruction note for the £23 million transfer, raised the alarm.

Anders fled the country on 29 June. She went via Singapore to Vancouver, Canada, and eventually got a cleaning job in Portland, Oregon. On the way she phoned friends to say that she had been called away. She asked one of them to look after her two cats.

Allen had also left the country – for Abu Dhabi – but he returned to Aberdeen a few weeks later. His wife confronted him about the affair. Allen denied it. Almost a year later, after their marriage had broken up, Allen's estranged wife reported her suspicions to the police. Allen was arrested and the search for Alison Anders intensified.

> WANTED: 31-year-old ACOL bridge player. Ex-bridge club chairman. Good organiser. Competent player except under pressure.

Anders returned to the United Kingdom in the company of two detectives. She and Roy Allen were found guilty of embezzling £23,332,996. After serving their prison sentences, they changed their names and moved to a rural location in Scotland. They may still be playing bridge.

Sometimes, when I'm dummy at a bridge club, I look around at the other people in the room and think of the interesting lives they must have led.

PLAYING TO LOSE?

YOKOHAMA, JAPAN, 1991

In the first 40 years of the Bermuda Bowl, the organisers tried various competition formats, but the nadir came in 1991, when the scheme for qualifying for the quarter-finals was open to abuse.

There were two qualifying groups of eight teams – Group E and Group W – and each team played seven matches. The group teams were ranked in order of total Victory Points. The top four of each group progressed to the quarter-finals, where knock-out matches featured the top team in Group E playing the fourth in Group W, the runners-up in Group E playing third in Group W and so on.

All went smoothly in Group W, but the last match of Group E highlighted the flaw in the scheme. Third-place Poland had already decided that they would prefer to play Iceland (the likely winners of Group W) in the quarter-finals, rather than European Champions Great Britain (almost certainly second in Group W).

Bridge Magazine covered the story:

> What the Poles had forgotten was that their last match would be against USA II. Now, USA II were also trying to finish fourth because they (foolish mortals!) preferred a quarter-final against Iceland to one against Great Britain. And they had a major advantage – they were *already* fourth, so whatever Poland attempted to hurl, they could simply pick up and hurl back.
>
> This at least leant [*sic*] some amusement to the final match. Poland in fact proved surprisingly inept at chucking points – one of them passed his partner's One Spade opening on a

fourteen-count, only to gain 6 IMPs when game proved to have no play at the other table. A Polish player absent-mindedly failed to go down in a cold slam which was not bid in the other room, to gain even more IMPs, and USA II emerged triumphant with a 9–21 loss.

The rules were changed for the next Bermuda Bowl. Teams finishing top of their group were allowed to choose which team from the other group's top four they wished to play.

THIRTEEN SPADES

DEVON, MAY 1993

Marcus Benorthan was partnering Brian Blades, and they were playing against their wives, Phyllis Benorthan and Ann Blades. It was a routine after-dinner evening of rubber bridge.

Brian Blades was the dealer for the sensational hand that became a big story in most British daily newspapers. It was the second deal of the evening. An old pack of cards had been thoroughly shuffled when Mr Blades took the cards and passed them across for the cut. Then he dealt the cards in the correct manner, one card at a time in a clockwise direction.

Marcus Benorthan watched the proceedings and then collected his hand. He had no need to sort his cards into suits. His first thought was that the other three had rigged the deal. Then he realised that they couldn't have, because he had watched the cards go through the normal procedure. In fact, he was the only person who had not touched the cards for that deal.

'Pass,' said Mr Blades, the dealer.

'One Heart,' said Mrs Blades.

'Stop, please. Seven Spades,' said Mr Benorthan.

'Pass,' said Mrs Benorthan.

'Pass,' said Mr Blades.

'Double,' said Mrs Blades.

'Redouble,' said Mr Benorthan.

The bid was passed out.

Phyllis Benorthan led a small heart. Her husband placed his thirteen spades on the table and claimed all thirteen tricks.

'With a hand like that you have to call a spade a spade,' Mr Benorthan was quoted as saying.

The Benorthans had been playing serious bridge for about sixteen years at that time. They played every day, including competitions at weekends. Mr Benorthan, a 67-year-old retired businessman, was also a bridge teacher.

The previous March, a man playing in a private club in Gateshead had dealt himself thirteen hearts.

BRAZIL VS. NORWAY

SANTIAGO, CHILE, 1993

The result of the Brazil–Norway World Championships semi-final depended on the last deal.

Dealer East. East–West Game.

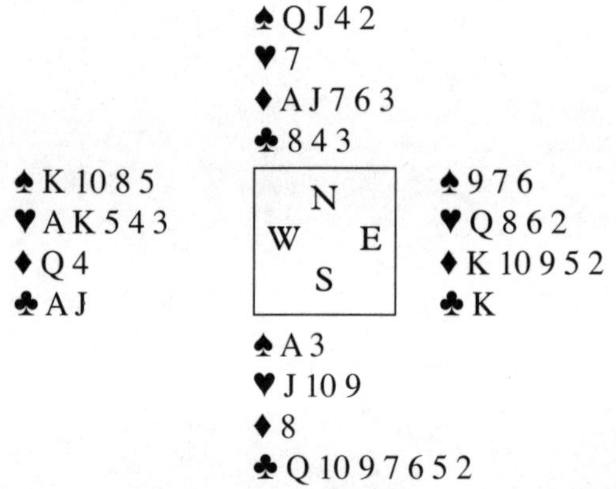

West	**North**	**East**	**South**
Brazil	*Norway*	*Brazil*	*Norway*
		Pass	3 ♣
Dble	5 ♣	Dble	All Pass

Both North–South partnerships ended in Five Clubs (doubled), but Norway miraculously made their contract. The swing of twelve IMPs gave Norway victory by three IMPs.

When the Norwegian South played this key hand, the Brazilian West led ♥A before assessing dummy. Declarer also took a long glance at his partner's offering. He has three possible losers, four if ♠K is badly positioned (as it is).

West continued with ♣A. His partner's king fell under the ace.

West can still rectify this by leading a second trump and taking away a cross-ruff. Instead he led a low spade and gave declarer a chance. The jack held the trick.

Declarer won ♠A, trumped a second heart, won ♦A, trumped a diamond, trumped the last heart, trumped a spade and then took out the last trump with his queen.

Contract made for 550 points.

Even the best can make mistakes.

The same board also provided a dramatic finale for the second semi-final, between USA II and Netherlands. Again both North–South partnerships played the hand in Five Clubs (doubled). Both declarers were two down for a loss of 300 points and Netherlands won the semi-final by three IMPs.

Netherlands beat Norway in the final.

THE CAT CONVENTION

WOLVERHAMPTON, 1993

The names of cats and dogs reveal a lot about owners. I know a physicist whose cats are called Newton and Schrödinger, and a music-lover who wants to call her next dog Offenbach. An American pole-vaulter, Stacy Dragila, has a dog called Sydney, in honour of where she won her Olympic gold medal.

So it is with bridge enthusiasts. One famous American player had three dogs called Finesse, Endplay and Deschapelles Coup. Another had poodles called Finesse and Ruff (but faced accusations of cheating when calling the dogs during a game). Other candidates for the bridge player's book of pet names are McKenney ('she was about to be discarded by some friends of ours') and Peter ('he's clever at defending himself'), but I have yet to hear anyone in the park calling, 'Stayman, stay.'

I once joined a foursome for rubber bridge on an evening when our hostess (my partner) was searching for a name for her black and white kitten. In the course of our best hand of the night, I bid 'Four No-trumps' and the kitten landed in our hostess's lap to claim far more attention than any ALERT card. The kitten was thus named Blackwood.

This featured hand, however, is set at the Wolverhampton Bridge Club, where the resident cat had been named Benjy after Benjaminised Acol, the club proprietor's favourite bidding system.

'This method, with its cheeky weak-two opening bids in the majors, has an annoying habit of getting in people's way – just like Benjy,' wrote Jane Bodin in *Bridge Plus Annual*, 1993.

Jane Bodin's tale took place during a match of some importance when bidding boxes were in use. This was the hand where Benjy did all the bidding. And strange bidding it was.

Dealer South. East–West Game.

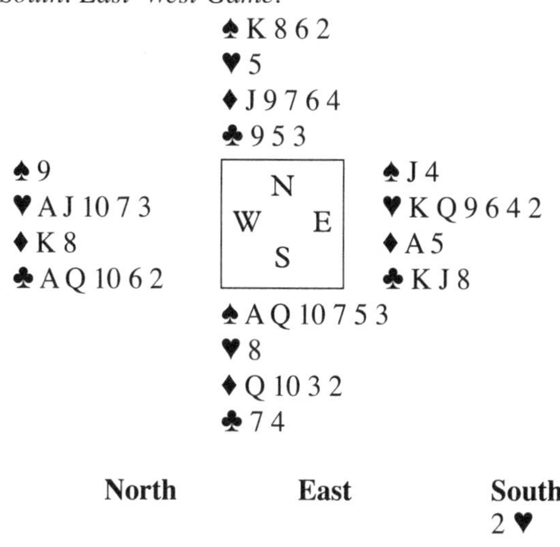

North: ♠ K 8 6 2 ♥ 5 ♦ J 9 7 6 4 ♣ 9 5 3

West: ♠ 9 ♥ A J 10 7 3 ♦ K 8 ♣ A Q 10 6 2

East: ♠ J 4 ♥ K Q 9 6 4 2 ♦ A 5 ♣ K J 8

South: ♠ A Q 10 7 5 3 ♥ 8 ♦ Q 10 3 2 ♣ 7 4

West	**North**	**East**	**South**
			2 ♥
All Pass			

As South attempted to extract the Two Spades card from her bidding box, Benjy the cat jumped on her lap, perhaps in the excitement of seeing such a perfect Benjy weak-two opener. The Two Hearts card fell on the table by mistake and the rules were clear that it had to stay there. The opposition's system did not permit a double on such holdings, so the hand was passed out.

South went seven off and East–West scored 350 points.

'But our opponents have a slam on,' North reflected, at the end of the play.

Indeed, most East–West partnerships would find Six Hearts for 1,430 points. All that could stop them would be a sacrifice of Six Spades (doubled), which costs 800 for four down, or a psychic bid from Benjy the cat.

EVERYBODY'S BEST FRIEND

NORWICH, 1995

Dr J H Merz of Norwich wrote to *Bridge Magazine* (July 1995) with details of a hand from a teams-of-four competition. It turned out that there was only one suit in the pack.

Dealer North. East–West Game.

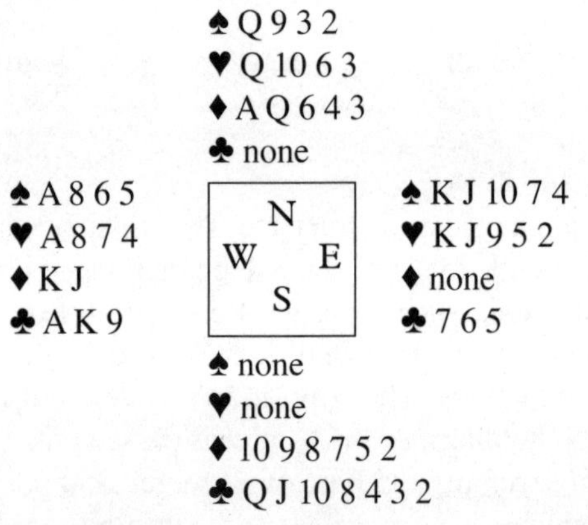

West	North	East	South
	Pass	Pass	1♦
2♦	3♦	4♦	5♦
6♦	7♦	Pass	Pass
Unknown			

The *Bridge Magazine* letter tantalisingly left the bidding open, allowing the reader to choose between doubling Seven Diamonds, bidding Seven Hearts or bidding Seven Spades, and also letting the reader unpack the various associated playing problems. The hand qualifies for strangeness, anyway, with seven successive logical bids of the same suit. East's bid of Four Diamonds was showing a singleton or void and asking West to select best major. West's response of Six Diamonds was asking East to choose.

With modern-day conventions, tournament players may not see this repetitive bidding of the same suit as particularly uncommon. In the 1991 European Championships, three players bid diamonds on Board 23 of the Israel–Poland match. The player who did not bid diamonds held ♦ A K Q 9 5 4.

One more unlikely bidding echo, however, is that envisaged by Patricia Fox Sheinwold in her book *Husbands and Other Men I've Played With* (1979). She imagines four men locked in a room in macho combat. The bidding goes something like this.

West	**North**	**East**	**South**
1 NT	2 NT	3 NT	4 NT
5 NT	6 NT	7 NT	8 NT

That has probably never happened, but we students of strangeness believe that anything is possible.

SEVERAL SWINGS

BEIJING, CHINA, OCTOBER 1995

Several unusually large swings came as a result of Board 58 in the quarter-finals of the 1995 Bermuda Bowl and Venice Cup competitions. Here is one example.

Dealer West. Game All.

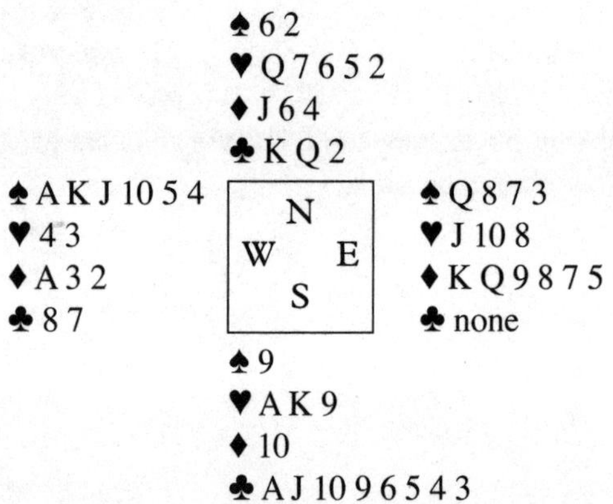

♠6 2
♥Q 7 6 5 2
♦J 6 4
♣K Q 2

♠A K J 10 5 4
♥4 3
♦A 3 2
♣8 7

♠Q 8 7 3
♥J 10 8
♦K Q 9 8 7 5
♣none

♠9
♥A K 9
♦10
♣A J 10 9 6 5 4 3

Open Room

West	**North**	**East**	**South**
Canada	*South Africa*	*Canada*	*South Africa*
1 ♠	Pass	2 ♦	3 ♣
3 ♠	5 ♣	5 ♠	6 ♣
Pass	Pass	6 ♠	All Pass

Closed Room

West	**North**	**East**	**South**
South Africa	*Canada*	*South Africa*	*Canada*
1 ♠	Pass	4 ♠	5 ♣
Pass	Pass	5 ♦	Pass
5 ♠	6 ♣	Dble	All Pass

In the Open Room, North led ♣K and Canada made all thirteen tricks for 1,460 points. In the Closed Room, West failed to cash the two aces and Canada made twelve tricks for 1,540 points. The swing to Canada was 3,000 points, or 22 IMPs. Not far away from the maximum of 24 IMPs.

Netherlands made a swing of seventeen IMPs on the same board. As East–West they bid Six Spades and made thirteen tricks (1,460 points). As North–South they successfully defended the same contract doubled to put it one off (another 200 points). Presumably they found the heart lead and follow-up.

In another match, on the same board, China's contract of Five Spades was doubled and a favourable lead brought thirteen tricks for 1,250 points. Opponents France played in Six Spades (doubled) and the resultant 1,860 points from thirteen tricks brought a swing of twelve IMPs.

THERE IS ALWAYS A FIRST TIME

OXFORD, 1995

This hand is familiar enough to be the first candidate for a book on non-strange bridge hands, but it threw up a lasting memory for North.

A relative newcomer to the game, North was learning the Stayman Convention. He had listened attentively when his partner explained how a response of Two Clubs asked if there was a four-card major in the other hand. Now North was eager to try the convention. Sure enough, the first hand of the evening was a good opportunity. Or so North thought.

Dealer East. Love All.

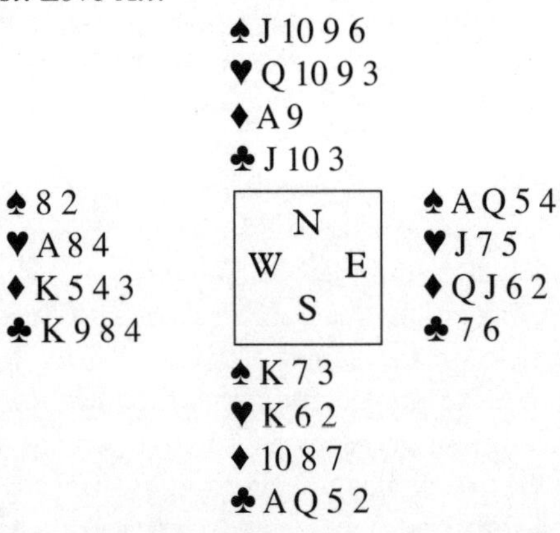

	North	
	♠ J 10 9 6 ♥ Q 10 9 3 ♦ A 9 ♣ J 10 3	
West ♠ 8 2 ♥ A 8 4 ♦ K 5 4 3 ♣ K 9 8 4	N W E S	**East** ♠ A Q 5 4 ♥ J 7 5 ♦ Q J 6 2 ♣ 7 6
	♠ K 7 3 ♥ K 6 2 ♦ 10 8 7 ♣ A Q 5 2	

West	North	East	South
		Pass	1 NT
Pass	2 ♣	Pass	2 ♦
Pass	2 NT	All Pass	

North's excitement at seeing two four-card majors momentarily overcame any concerns about the strength of his hand. As soon as the bid came out, however, he remembered his partner's rider: *You really need ten or more points to explore with Stayman over a weak No-trump.*

As might be expected, the god of bridge teachers decreed that there was no lucky four–four fit. A flustered North tried to escape into Two No-trumps and then laid down his hand sheepishly.

'Sorry, partner,' he said. 'But I've got three tens and three nines, if that's any help.'

South surveyed the hand thoughtfully. 'Thank you, partner,' he said bitterly. 'I'll use the three nines to call the emergency services.'

South made a plucky attempt but went one off.

North remembered that hand for ever.

In 1993 there was a challenge match (Burgay vs. Stayman) between teams playing different systems over a One No-trump opener. A computer was programmed to generate an assortment of hands in which the dealer had a sixteen–eighteen One No-trump opener. The Stayman team used traditional methods while the Burgay team used a system devised by television producer Leandro Burgay. The problem is that the results of such challenge matches rarely provide a clear-cut conclusion. It may be the play of the hand by the participants that determines the outcome.

The Stayman Convention was named after Sam Stayman, who wrote the first article on the subject (*Bridge World*, June 1945). Stayman credits George Rapée with the first use of the form, although Ewart Kempson and Jack Marx used similar systems in Britain in the 1930s. Marx was unable to publish his system until 1946 because British bridge publications were suspended during a period of paper shortage.

'That the convention now generally bears his [Stayman's] name is a tribute to American advertising genius, though it was born British,' wrote Rhoda Barrow (*Bridge Magazine*, April 1971).

PASSING WITH OVER TWENTY POINTS – LESSON 3

SCHWENNINGEN, GERMANY, FEBRUARY 1996

This hand occurred in an international bridge tournament.

Dealer South. Game All.

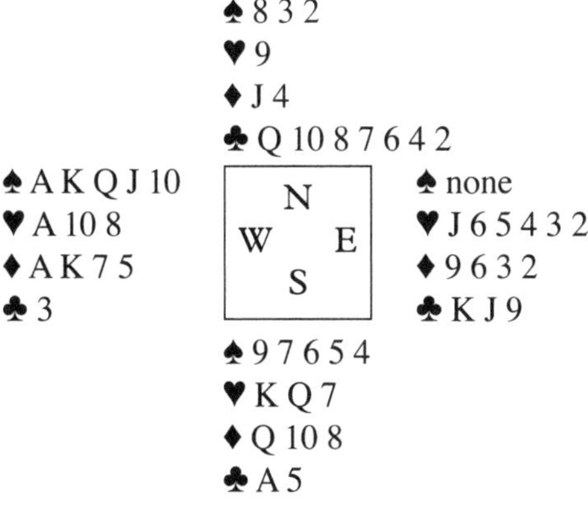

South	West	North	East
1 ♠	All Pass		

West studied his meagre holding of 21 points and decided to pass. Declarer won three tricks and East–West scored 400 points.

In the other room, East–West's Five Hearts went one off for 100 points to North–South.

Well, they say that Pass is the best bid in the book.

A TOURNAMENT FREAK

TUNISIA, OCTOBER 1997

Freak hands have a deadly presence in tournaments. This one is from the 1997 Transnational Teams World Championship.

Dealer South. Love All.

	North	
	♠ 7 6 ♥ J 10 9 8 7 5 4 3 ♦ 9 2 ♣ 3	
West ♠ A K Q J 10 9 8 5 4 3 ♥ K ♦ K 3 ♣ none	N W E S	**East** ♠ 2 ♥ none ♦ 4 ♣ A K Q 10 9 8 7 6 5 4 2
	♠ none ♥ A Q 6 2 ♦ A Q J 10 8 7 6 5 ♣ J	

Table 1

West	North	East	South
			1 ♦
Pass	1 ♥	Pass	4 ♣
4 ♠	Pass	6 ♣	6 ♦
6 ♠	Pass	7 ♣	7 ♦
All Pass			

Table 2

West	**North**	**East**	**South**
			1 ♦
5 ♠	Pass	6 ♣	Dble
6 ♠	Pass	Pass	Dble
All Pass			

At Table 1, declarer was one away when West led a top spade (minus 50). Seven Diamonds on an eight–two fit is a better sacrifice than Seven Hearts on an eight–four fit, against which East can lead two clubs to promote a trump trick for West.

At Table 2, North led a diamond to South's ace. South was unable to take out dummy's singleton trump, so declarer was able to trump the heart, make ♦K and succeed with the contract (plus 1,200). Declarer would have gone down if North had led a trump.

THE ONE–ONE FIT

CHICAGO, ILLINOIS, 1998

Board 55 of the 1998 Spingold Trophy semi-final not only helped to settle the outcome of the match but produced an unusual event – one North–South pair played their contract in a one–one fit.

Dealer North. Game All.

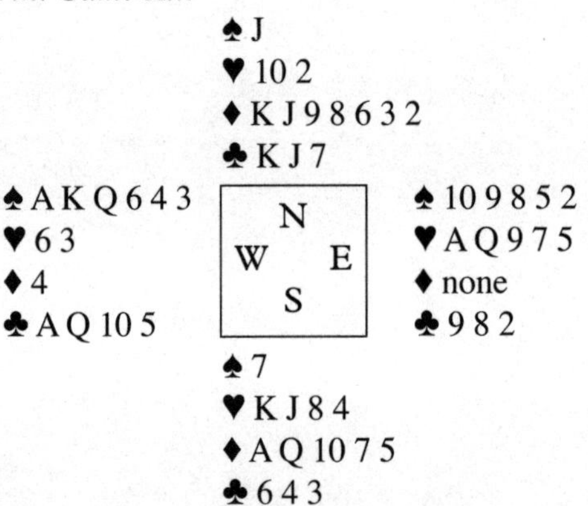

Closed Room

West	**North**	**East**	**South**
	3 ♦	Pass	3 ♠
Pass	4 ♠	All Pass	

Open Room

West	**North**	**East**	**South**
	Pass	Pass	1 ♦
4 ♠	5 ♦	5 ♥	Dble
Pass	Pass	5 ♠	Pass
Pass	6 ♦	6 ♠	Pass
Pass	Dble	All Pass	

The Open Room contract of Six Spades was one off for a gain of 200 to North–South.

In the Closed Room, South's Three Spades was a psychic bid aimed at preventing opponents from finding their spade fit. Well, that certainly happened. If North–South were looking to escape into Five Diamonds when the spade contract was doubled, they didn't have a chance. East–West were happy to take the undoubled penalty. In fact the contract was eight down for 800 points to East–West and a swing of fourteen IMPs. It would not have looked so bad had East–West played in Four Spades at the other table (and scored 650 points).

The match was decided by one IMP after a recount.

THE FREAKIEST HAND

GOLD CUP, 1999

This hand was described by Andrew Robson, bridge correspondent for *The Times*, as 'by far the freakiest hand that I have ever (and, almost certainly, will ever) come across'. It is a rare hand that has seven voids.

This freak, like most freaks, required guesswork and flair. The only convention of value is the Unconventional Convention. South's bidding worked out well.

Dealer West. North–South Game.

	North	
	♠ 4 3 ♥ none ♦ A J 10 9 8 7 6 5 4 3 2 ♣ none	
West ♠ none ♥ A 10 9 8 7 6 5 4 3 2 ♦ K Q ♣ A	N W E S	**East** ♠ none ♥ Q ♦ none ♣ K Q J 10 9 8 7 6 5 4 3 2
	♠ A K Q J 10 9 8 7 6 5 2 ♥ K J ♦ none ♣ none	

West	**North**	**East**	**South**
4 ♥	5 ♦	7 ♣	7 ♠
Dble	All Pass		

East decided that he was only going to pick up a twelve-card suit once in his lifetime, so he plumped for Seven Clubs. Then he was upstaged by South. West led ♣A and dummy was revealed. Even the most sober of bridge declarers would have had trouble keeping a straight face.

Thank you, partner.

Declarer trumped the opening lead in dummy and discarded a heart from hand. A second heart was thrown away on the ♦A and declarer tabled the rest of his cards.

ZIA MAHMOOD AGAINST SEVEN COMPUTERS

LONDON, SEPTEMBER 1999

The ultimate challenge between bridge player and bridge computer took place when Zia Mahmood and seven computers met over two days in September 1999. Marc Smith wrote up the story of the contest in *Man vs Machine* (1999).

People had been developing computer software for many years. In the early days, the standard joke was that computers needed to improve their bridge to become hopeless. Gradually, they became technically better and better, but they lacked the psychological make-up of bridge stars. Computers do not get tired or nervous, but they cannot handle improvisation easily and their rapport with a partner is difficult to develop. On the other hand, they play fast and have never been accused of signalling to partner with feet or fingers.

Playing against Zia Mahmood was as big a challenge as computers could expect to face (if they were capable of expecting and had faces). The charismatic Zia was not only one of the best players in the world but one of the most intuitive and innovative. When Zia published *Bridge My Way* (1991), he offered to take a bet of £1 million that no computer would be able to beat him at bridge. The bet was withdrawn several years later, but the stake for Man vs. Machine, in September 1999, was $10,000 (over £6,000).

At Andrew Robson's London club, the eight competitors – seven computers and one man – played a series of matches in teams of four. The first nine matches lasted seven deals, and the remaining matches five deals apiece (because time was running out). Partners and team-mates changed after each match. Teams scored a point for each deal won – half a point for a flat board – and the first team to four points (three points if there were only five deals) won one Victory Point for winning the match. The first player to reach ten Victory Points won the overall contest.

It took fifteen matches to find a winner and the final table of Victory Points read as follows: Zia Mahmood (ten), Oxford Bridge (eight), Blue Chip Bridge (eight), Q-plus Bridge (eight), Saitek Pro Bridge 500 (eight), Meadowlark Bridge (seven), Micro Bridge (six) and GIB (five).

That the GIB computer finished bottom was a surprise given that GIB had won the 1998 World Computer Bridge Championships and was soon to defend its title successfully in 2000.

Zia Mahmood was a fairly passive observer on this hand – the first of Match 12 – when he was only one Victory Point in the lead.

Dealer East. Love All.

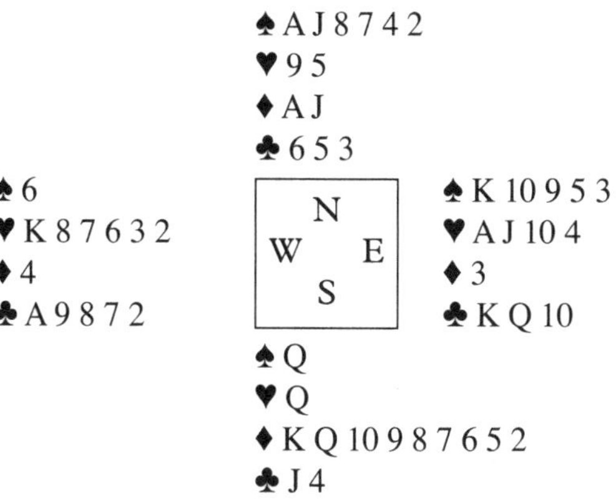

Closed Room

West	**North**	**East**	**South**
Saitek	*GIB*	*Micro Bridge*	*Blue Chip*
		1 ♠	4 ♦
4 ♥	All Pass		

Open Room

West	**North**	**East**	**South**
Oxford	*Zia*	*Meadowlark*	*Q-plus*
		1 ♠	3 ♦
3 ♥	Pass	4 ♥	5 ♦
Dble	All Pass		

The Saitek computer software made eleven tricks for 450 points in the Closed Room. For Zia to win a point on the board, all Q-plus needed to do was not go too many down in the Open Room. Oxford Bridge led the singleton spade, which was won by dummy's ace. Declarer played ♦J from dummy and this held the trick. This was followed by a spade ruff and a club to East's ten. For some reason, East led back a small spade. Declarer threw away the remaining club and made Five Diamonds (doubled) for 550 points.

INTERNATIONAL BANNED FOR CHEATING

WALES, DECEMBER 1999

The issue of cheating returned to the agenda in 1999 when Wales international Tony Haworth was banned from tournament bridge for ten years after being found guilty of introducing prepared hands into the Welsh Foursomes tournament the previous September. At a hearing of the laws and ethics committee of the Welsh Bridge Union, it was alleged that Haworth had substituted his own pack on at least four occasions and dealt the cards without shuffling. His team was disqualified from the Welsh Foursomes tournament.

'Five witnesses said Mr Haworth, of Porthcawl, Mid Glamorgan, would arrive at the table early, replace one of the packs with his own, then deal them without shuffling,' reported the *Daily Telegraph*.

It was the first time the Welsh Bridge Union had banned a player for cheating in their 50-year history. Haworth had represented Wales on eleven occasions and had previously been non-playing captain of the Wales team. His ban prevented him from playing tournament bridge anywhere in the world, but did not exclude him from social bridge.

Accusations like the Buenos Aires Affair (see pages 142 to 147) and the Bermuda Incident (see page 172) focus on how partners may be able to cheat by communicating subtly with each other. The Haworth case was that of one person acting alone, and Haworth made it clear that his partner had no awareness of what was happening.

Packs have been switched elsewhere, and other examples of players caught cheating while acting alone include those trying to alter score slips in their favour and those who use gamesmanship involving the director. The most blatant method of cheating is the player who leans back to look at opponents' cards or even knocks something on to the floor to improve the vision of opponent's hand. Alternatively some players try to hear conversations at the next table in a duplicate competition.

The big question in Haworth's case is why a top-class player should set up a few hands that will enable him to do better at one of the smaller tournaments, especially a tournament where the person has three other non-cheating team-mates.

People have tried to answer this question. Some suggest that the desire to win becomes obsessive. Others believe that cheaters simply wish to impress a girlfriend or even their bridge partner.

Fifteen months after Haworth's suspension, the American Contract Bridge League suspended a player for eighteen months because of card manipulation during the shuffle and deal. The player was found guilty of giving his partner a specific card when he was dealer. The player in question protested his innocence – he said he was just a clumsy dealer because of a serious finger disability – and the legal ramifications threaten to run and run.

A NEW FORM OF BRIDGE, A NEW FORM OF CHEATING?

THE INTERNET, 1999

One night in 1975, when I was a postgraduate student in Canada, I received a phone call inviting me to log on to my nearest computer. I followed instructions until I linked up with two other postgraduates and a computer operator who was developing a bridge program.

I cackled with laughter at the 'computer names' of the other three and entered a nickname that I knew the others would recognise – 'Mate'. The concept was exciting, even if it did take us 40 minutes to bid and play the first hand.

On the second hand someone revoked. It sent the program into an everlasting loop that kept playing one particular trick beyond our control.

The telephone rang and I walked along a corridor to answer it.

'Sorry, Mate,' said the voice at the other end. 'We've got a glitch. There's still a bit of work to do on this one.'

Plenty of work has been done in the years since. The Internet has captured the hearts – or the spades – of many bridge players. There are now plenty of options for logging on and finding a game with players from all round the world. Kibitzers can watch in 'spectator mode' and players can play without travelling and without worrying about whether the church-hall heating has been turned on. Smokers can smoke without upsetting anyone else, and there's always a game going at 3 a.m. Some people play when their spouse is away and some play when their spouse is at home. Players can chat to each other or they can restrict socialising to shorthand messages such as 'TYP' (Thank you, partner) and 'GJP' (Good job, partner). And they can compete with the best throughout the world in competitions like the Internet World Championships.

Sadly, though, the Internet brings new ideas for cheating.

As we have seen, bridge historians have documented a number of ways in which a player may cheat, some of which have been borne out in practice and others of which have not. We have polished tables, mirrors, special glasses and marked cards, special ways of stacking cards, pack switching, canny shuffling, and conveying messages to partner by whistling, singing, finger tapping, pencil pointing, foot rubbing, ear scratching, syllable stressing, facial grimacing and lipreading. One of the Marx Brothers, Chico, always joked about the most straightforward system of all: 'If you like my lead, don't bother to signal with a high card. Just smile and nod your head.'

Some tactics push play to the limits of ethics, like suddenly disturbing the rhythm of playing a suit in an effort to force a revoke or deliberately hesitating in order to give partner information. Then there is the story of the player who deliberately called out of turn when he saw his partner heading for an unmakable slam; the director forced his partner to stop bidding at game level.

In rubber bridge, where good cards are more essential, some players have cheated by stacking cards. They gather each trick in such a way that each set of four cards is stacked high–low–high–low. With minimal shuffling the cards can be arranged suitably and partner can be shown where to cut.

Another method is to use something like a ring to mark the aces and kings and then slip the marked cards into the right hands. Then there was the player who marked the cards with ink that was invisible to the naked eye but could be spotted through special dark glasses.

By taking away face-to-face contact and eliminating playing cards, the Internet protects players from some traditional forms of cheating. It brings its own problems, however, like the people who sign up for the same game as East under one name and West under another name (using two computers). An Internet competition late in 1999 raised some questions. The story was summarised by Jan van Cleeff in *NRC Handelsblad* and translated by Onno Eskes. Naturally I learned of this on the Internet.

In the competition in question, a team of non-experts beat a team of renowned experts in a semi-final.

'I had a very unpleasant feeling about the match,' one of the experts was quoted as saying afterwards. 'They [our opponents] didn't play great, but at the critical moments they made some remarkably good decisions. Their play was sometimes so unlikely that it literally makes me sick.'

An international conducts and ethics committee was formed, and the finger pointed at one particular player who had made more than twenty remarkable play-and-bid decisions. This particular person, tagged 'Mrs Smith', was found guilty of playing with 'unauthorised information'.

But how was it done?

'Maybe Mrs Smith had two computers at her disposal,' wrote Jan van Cleeff. 'The first one she uses to log on as a player, the second to log on as a spectator. That would allow her to see all the hands of the deal she is playing at the same time. Or she makes a phone call to a friend who has a computer and logs on as a spectator…'

ISRAEL AND PALESTINE

MAASTRICHT, HOLLAND, MARCH 2000

The history of sports and games is littered with examples of matches played at a time of political unrest. A few have increased tension (e.g. the Hungary–Soviet Union water-polo battle at the 1956 Olympics and the El Salvador–Honduras soccer World Cup qualifier of 1969) but the majority pass peacefully. This bridge match, in the fourth round of the Transnational Mixed Team Championships, was an example of the latter. It was reputedly the first time that teams representing Israel and Palestine had met in any kind of sporting contest.

The Palestine Bridge Federation was founded in 1995. Five years later it had about 100 members, representing most of the main cities of the West Bank and East Jerusalem. Three of their six-person squad came from East Jerusalem and the others from Ramalla, Nablus and Bethlehem. The four Israelis were from Tel Aviv (two), Petah Tikva and Givatayim.

The powerful Israeli team were the favourites to win the match, but the outcome was closer than anticipated. A low-scoring match ended 18–12 Victory Points in favour of Israel.

The bidding and play for this hand was the same at each table, but the hand has one interesting question: Should East–West sacrifice in Seven Diamonds (despite the unfavourable vulnerability)?

Dealer North. East–West Game.

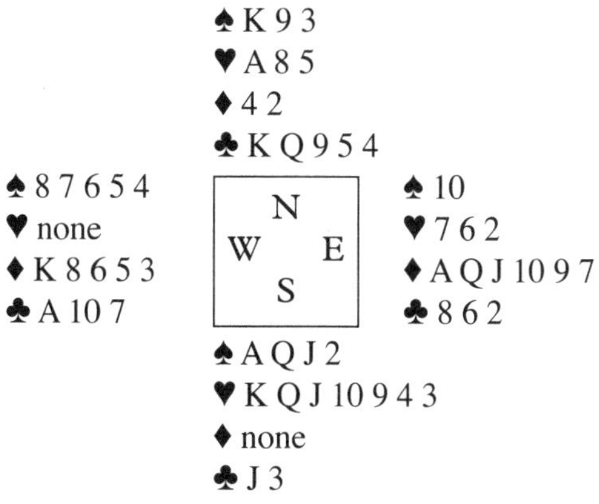

West	**North**	**East**	**South**
	1 ♣	2 ♦	2 ♥
5 ♦	Pass	Pass	6 ♥
All Pass			

Both Wests led a diamond and both Souths had little trouble making Six Hearts with a diamond ruff, three rounds of trumps, four top spades, one club (after losing to ♣A) and three more hearts. Six Hearts scored 980 points.

The strange thing was that Seven Diamonds went either three off (on an unlikely club lead) or two off on any other lead (if dummy's fifth spade is cannily set up). Assuming the contract was doubled, the sacrifice would have cost either 800 points or 500 points.

As Andrew Robson commented, after reviewing the hand in *The Times* (25 June 2001): 'You will probably only rarely see an example of a profitable sacrifice of Seven over Six when you are vulnerable and your opponents are not.'

HOUSE OF LORDS VS. HOUSE OF COMMONS

LONDON, APRIL 2000

The list of bridge-playing politicians is a long one. The most famous are probably Dwight Eisenhower of the United States and Deng Xiaoping of China, whose only official title at the time of his death was President of the Chinese Bridge Federation. Winston Churchill learned to play the game in 1902, in Cairo, where he played at least four rubbers a night.

According to Randolph Churchill, however, in *Winston S. Churchill: Young Statesman, 1901–14* (1967), politicians do not usually make good bridge players:

> Churchill, Asquith and Birkenhead were all duffers and consistent losers. It may be that politicians, who tend to be wilful men of action, always want to play the hand and overbid. They like one-man shows and not partnerships. Of course there have been exceptions. Bonar Law was competent if pedestrian, Duff Cooper good if erratic. In our day and age we have the brilliant exception of Mr Iain MacLeod, who is one of the four best bridge players in the country and has written a book called *Bridge is an Easy Game* [1952].

MacLeod, Chancellor of the Exchequer in Harold Wilson's Labour government, was undoubtedly a top player. 'Iain's transformation from bridge layabout to cabinet minister, very nearly Prime Minister, was quite remarkable,' wrote Terence Reese in *Bridge at the Top* (1977).

The annual match between the House of Lords and the House of Commons began in 1975. In the early days the hands were duplicated but the scoring was more akin to rubber bridge. Some very good players have taken part over the years, including Harold Lever, who, in the late 1970s, switched sides from the Commons to the Lords.

In 1984 the Duke of Atholl led a winning British Parliamentary Team against the United States Congress in Washington, DC, and the British politicians won a return match. Six years later the UK Parliamentarians played against a team of American billionaires known as the US Tycoons or 'Corporate America'. The tycoons were too strong for the British politicians.

The Lords–Commons match of 2000 tied the series at 13–13, with a win for the Commons. The result hinged on the outcome of the first board of the match.

Ah, the first board.

There are plenty of strange stories about first boards. Players are settling into their seats, sizing up their partner's mood, assessing their own sense of occasion. It is natural to be nervous, and some can be flustered.

Is it better to defend the first hand, watch partner play or play a hand as soon as possible? How should bridge players warm up before the start?

Even the best can take some time to accustom themselves to a strange environment. Consider Boris Schapiro at the start of the 1949 European Championships. He was playing for holders Great Britain against Denmark when he opened One Diamond out of turn on the first hand because he was unfamiliar with the type of board being used. When his partner was prevented from calling, Schapiro guessed the contract at Five Diamonds and escaped with no swing.

There are many examples of the first board deciding the match, and the 26th match of the Lords–Commons series was one of them. Bridget Prentice, the Labour MP for Lewisham East, arrived in good time but at the wrong place. The Portland Club had moved to new premises in Brook Street.

After a taxi ride across town, she arrived breathless and was thrown into the limelight on the first board. Her partner, Dr John Marek, had represented Wales in Camrose Cup matches.

Dealer East. East–West Game.

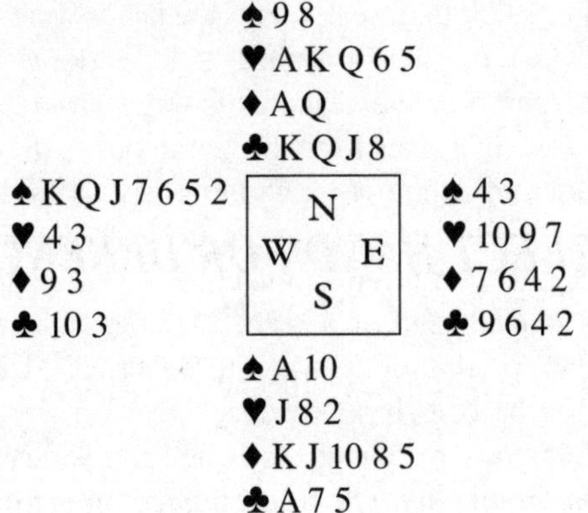

West	**North**	**East**	**South**
	Marek		*Prentice*
		Pass	1 NT
2 ♠	4 NT	Pass	5 ♥
Pass	7 NT	Pass	Pass
Dble	All Pass		

Seven No-trumps (doubled) was a lay-down. When the House of Lords were North–South, the bidding stopped at Six Hearts. This first hand was a match decider.

In Lords–Commons matches, the last hand can be as tense as the first. There are stories of Members of Parliament dashing back for the division bell on a three-line party whip, which forces them to vote.

The match in 2000 was a watershed in Parliamentary history. The reform of the House of Lords and the reduction of the number of hereditary peers meant that most of the 2000 Lords team would be unable to continue. Observers feared that the Lords would become the weaker of the two teams. One cynic even suggested that this might have been the true reason for the reforms.

A PERFECT HAND FOR DEFENCE

USA, 2000

According to *The ACBL Bulletin*, a tournament director saw these cards dealt and the correct protocol was followed. Svend Novrup reconstructed the hand in *Bridge Plus* (1 April 2000). Seven Diamonds (redoubled) was outscored by this sacrifice. South assumed that North's bid of Seven Spades (showing first-round diamond control) meant ♦A rather than a void. West led ♦2 and claimed the rest. Minus 3,800.

Dealer East. Game All.

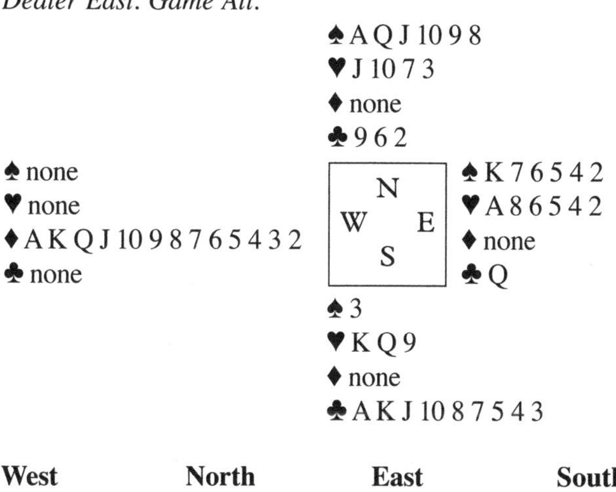

North:
♠A Q J 10 9 8
♥J 10 7 3
♦ none
♣9 6 2

West:
♠ none
♥ none
♦A K Q J 10 9 8 7 6 5 4 3 2
♣ none

East:
♠K 7 6 5 4 2
♥A 8 6 5 4 2
♦ none
♣Q

South:
♠3
♥K Q 9
♦ none
♣A K J 10 8 7 5 4 3

West	**North**	**East**	**South**
		Pass	2 ♣
7 ♦	7 ♠	Dble	7 NT
Dble	All Pass		

THROWN OUT

WALES, 2000

This type of strange hand occasionally appears on duplicate night. It is the one that produces a variety of contracts at all levels and yet two foursomes somehow pass it out.

Dealer West. Love All.

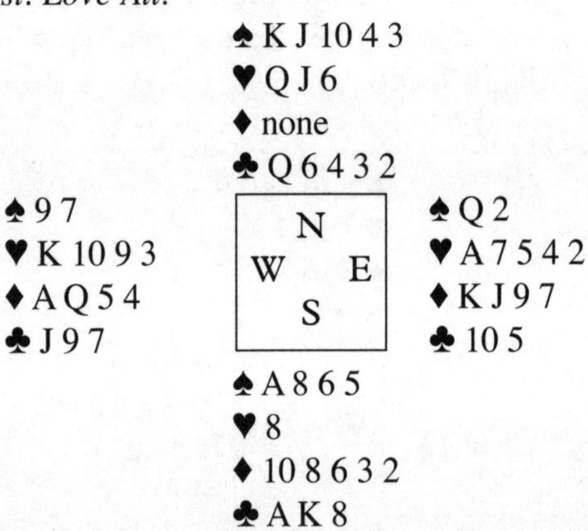

The scoresheet included Three Hearts by East–West and Four Spades by North–South (making twelve). On two occasions the hand had been passed out.

'Passed out?' said one player. 'It must have been a comment on partner fainting after seeing the cards.'

'One North couldn't decide whether to write *passed out or thrown in*,' said North. 'He's written *thrown out*.'

STRANGE CONVERSATIONS

DERBYSHIRE, 2000

The scene was a four-table Howell movement in a small room at the back of the chapel hall. The choir next door was rehearsing songs from *West Side Story* and the refrain of 'One Heart' provided an interesting background to the game.

It was a very friendly club, the type where, 'Any questions?' meant, 'Who's for tea and who's for coffee?'

The director's partner was in charge of the bell for signalling the table movements and start of play.

'Ring the bell,' said the director.

'I just did. Nobody heard me.'

The director shouted across the room, 'Could you make your noise a little more quietly, please.'

The director's partner rang the bell again.

The club had not invested in bidding boxes yet, even though two or three of its members were a little deaf. It led to some comical bidding sequences. The misunderstandings sometimes lasted until the end of the hand.

This hand is taken from a typical evening's bridge. It is not a particularly strange hand in itself, but is here as a reminder that conversation at the bridge table can be as unique as the hands.

Dealer South. Love All.

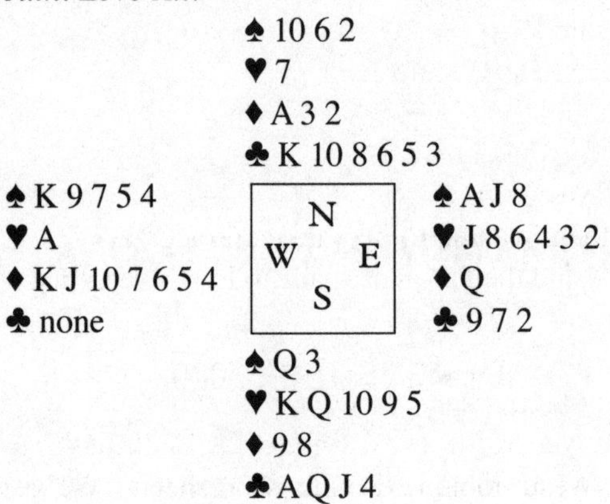

'Three Hearts,' said East. He had to repeat it a couple of times.

'Double,' said South.

No one asked what the double meant.

'Four Diamonds,' said West.

'Four Clubs,' said North.

'You can't bid Four Clubs,' said East.

'Oh, can I pass then?'

The four players ummed and aahed and laughed about the ethics of this. It did not take long. A woman with charm and beauty was sitting North. The pass was upheld.

'As it's my turn for two bids,' said East. 'I pass twice.'

'Five Clubs,' said South.

'Oh, come on, that's using information,' said East and West simultaneously.

'Oh, no. I would bid that anyway,' said South, another beautiful woman. 'Anyway, I haven't had a day off for six weeks.'

The choir was singing 'I want to be in America'.

'You can have another bid if you want,' said East.

'Five Hearts,' said West.

'Five Hearts?' asked North, unsure she had heard properly.

'You can't bid Five Hearts,' said East. 'My partner's just bid that.'

'I was asking him if he'd bid Five Hearts,' said North. 'Six Clubs.'

'Ugh,' said South.

It was passed out.

'My lead,' said West.

'No, no, no. My lead,' said East.

'South bid clubs first.'

'They both bid clubs first.'

'Oh, no. Who's going to play it?'

Neither of them wanted to play the contract.

West led ♥A and then a small spade to East's ace. East's ♠K won the last trick.

Two off.

'Did we double, partner?' asked West.

'I thought it was one of my last two bids,' said East.

'Oh,' said West, looking at the scoresheet. 'We've got Six Diamonds on.'

This is not a particularly strange conversation, but a reminder of all those weird discussions we have heard at the table. One duplicate night I arrived at a table just as a player was knocking his bidding box on the floor and tipping up his tea.

'You must have been in the King's Arms before you came here,' his partner said.

'No,' he replied. 'I finessed the King's Arms this evening.'

Another time I heard a young mother telling an older lady about her children.

'My boy's eleven and my daughter's two years younger. Do you have children?'

'Two,' the old lady said. 'Both boys. The eldest is seventy-one but the youngest is not yet seventy. Both retired of course.'

Another lady in her nineties, somewhat deaf, had a habit of shouting her post-mortems at her long-suffering partner.

'You should have led a club,' she shouted one night.

'I should have led a club,' her partner yelled back, in a comic loud voice that all 40-odd members could hear.

DENMARK VS SPAIN

TENERIFE, 2001

One of the biggest swings in team play occurred when Denmark played Spain in the 2001 European Championships. On Board 14, Denmark made Six Spades (doubled) when East–West and Six Hearts (doubled) when North–South.

Dealer North. Love All.

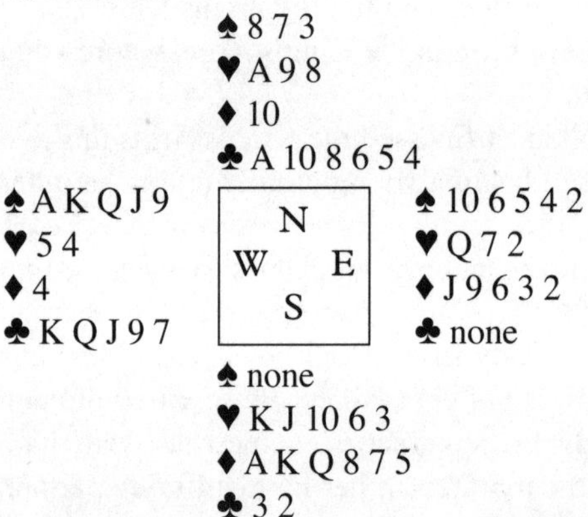

Open Room

West	**North**	**East**	**South**
Denmark	*Spain*	*Denmark*	*Spain*
	Pass	Pass	2 ♠ (i)
3 ♠	4 ♥	4 ♠	5 ♥
5 ♠	Pass	Pass	6 ♥
Pass	Pass	6 ♠	Dble
All Pass			

(i) Shows an opening bid with at least five–five in the red suits

Closed Room

West	**North**	**East**	**South**
Spain	*Denmark*	*Spain*	*Denmark*
	Pass	Pass	1 ♥
2 ♥	3 ♥	3 ♠	4 ♥
4 ♠	Pass	Pass	5 ♦
5 ♠	Pass	Pass	6 ♥
Pass	Pass	Dble	All Pass

In the Open Room, against Six Spades (doubled), North led ♣A rather than one of his partner's two red suits. He was expecting either East or West to have a heart shortage, and hoped to catch partner with a singleton club. Declarer ruffed, crossed to a top trump and saw South discard. Declarer discarded three hearts on three top clubs and then led ♦J, forcing South to win his ace. A diamond return was ruffed and declarer cross-ruffed the last five tricks. Plus 1,210.

In the Closed Room, West led ♠A. Declarer ruffed and played a low heart to the ace. Then he led ♦10.

'East should have covered with the jack, so promoting his nine (and defeating the contract),' wrote Andrew Robson in *The Times*. 'When he played low, declarer, reasoning that East held the diamond length (West had shown five spades and a five-card minor which had to be clubs to offer any hope), elected to play low from hand.'

'A Chinese finesse by a Dane against a Spaniard in Tenerife,' said Zia Mahmood, writing in the *Guardian*.

Declarer now played a heart to the jack and that finesse worked too. He ruffed a low diamond, ruffed a spade, won ♥K, dropping the queen, and then cashed four diamonds and ♣A, leaving a club loser at the end. Another 1,210 to Denmark.

Denmark gained twenty IMPs on the board and went on to win the match 57–18 (23–7 in Victory Points).

TWO-PERSON BRIDGE

OXFORD, OCTOBER 2001

Under the heading 'Honeymoon Bridge', *The Bridge Players' Encyclopedia* lists three forms of the two-person game. My personal favourite is a variant of these. I shall describe it briefly.

Two players sit in adjacent seats and four hands are dealt as normal. Each player looks at all the cards in one hand ('the known hand') and seven cards in the hand opposite ('the surprise hand'). The contents of the known hand and the surprise hand are not revealed to opponent. Dealer bids first and the bidding ends after one pass. Defender leads from the known hand before looking at the unknown cards in the surprise hand. After the opening lead, defender is in a position to play 'best defence' by playing cards from both hands without showing them to declarer. Declarer plays the contract from the known hand, with the surprise hand now exposed as dummy.

I find this variant works best with a goulash deal. Otherwise, players rarely risk game contracts with the possibility of facing breathtaking double-dummy defence after a double. It is more common for a hand to be passed out and slams are rare.

Would you, dealer and vulnerable, bid slam on the following holding?

Surprise Hand
♠ A J 5
♥ none
♦ Q 10 8
♣ 6

Known Hand
♠9
♥A K Q 9 8 3 2
♦K 7 4
♣4 3

Dealer knows the approximate value of the exposed twenty cards (nineteen high-card points plus good distribution in the known hand) and has to guess at the six unknown cards.

The expected number of points still to be revealed in these six cards is (6 x 21)/32 = four. The expected number of hearts is (6 x 6)/32 = one. Working on expectation, the best guess we can make of the surprise hand is therefore:

♠A J x x x
♥x
♦Q 10 x x
♣A x x

This would result at least one diamond loser and an almost certain club loser. Four Hearts is the sensible contract. After all, there's only a combined total of 23 points predicted.

Naturally, dealer reasoned differently: *I'm behind in the scoring and need a vulnerable slam to make up ground. On the last hand I bid Five Diamonds and made all thirteen tricks. I don't want to miss out again, and this dummy is shaping up nicely. The ♠A opposite my singleton is a dream card. If I can fluke another six or seven points and a couple of hearts in dummy, I'll be home and dry. I've only got two or three losers as it stands. If it all goes pear-shaped, I'll blame my partner.*

Dealer South. Game All.

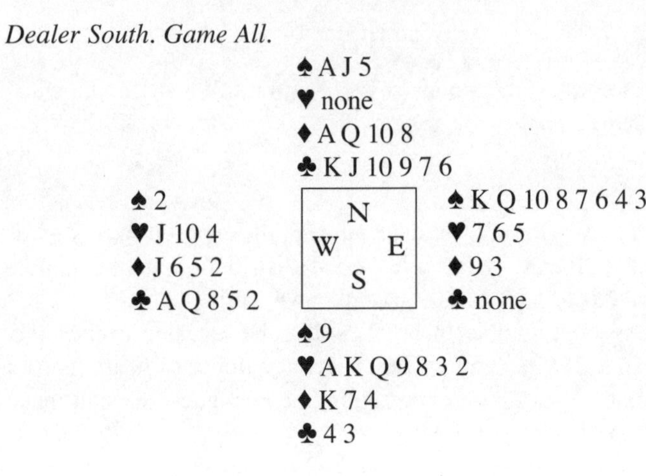

South	West
6♥	Pass

Defender led a singleton spade knowing that partner had ♠K but not knowing about the club void (until he looked at his surprise hand's other six cards).

For some reason declarer returned to hand with ♦K rather than the (safer) spade option (which would have been overruffed). Three top hearts collected all the trumps. Declarer led an extra heart, discarding a club from dummy, and then went across to ♦A before returning to hand by ruffing a spade. Then declarer led a small diamond. He willed the diamonds to split three–three instead of taking the finesse. When diamonds did not split he came back to hand with another spade ruff and then led a small club. Fortunately West had the ace and the slam was made.

Other forms of the two-handed game include double-dummy, semi-exposed dummy and 'draw bridge'.

Double dummy is where four hands are dealt face down and then the two players look at their own hand and bid. After the bidding, the two dummies are exposed and play commences.

In the semi-exposed form, seven cards of each dummy are exposed and each player can see these cards before bidding.

'Draw bridge' has various forms. Players receive thirteen cards apiece and then compete for the chance to replace a card with one of the spare cards. Each player is left with a full hand, and a game more akin to knock-out whist can then take place.

THE APPEAL THAT DECIDED THE REISINGER TROPHY

USA, 2001

Bridge has many strange features, including the requirement to declare bidding strategy, its appeals system and the hiding of tournament opponents from each other by screens. This example concerns the last two of these.

The score of a bridge match (sometimes the result) can be decided later by an appeal against the ruling on one particular hand. Results of horseraces, athletic competitions and Grand Prix can also be changed by appeals and disqualifications, but match scores are rarely altered. Bridge committees have the power to add and subtract from the scores.

Here is an example from a top American tournament, the Reisinger Trophy. This was Board 14 of the final.

Dealer East. Love All.

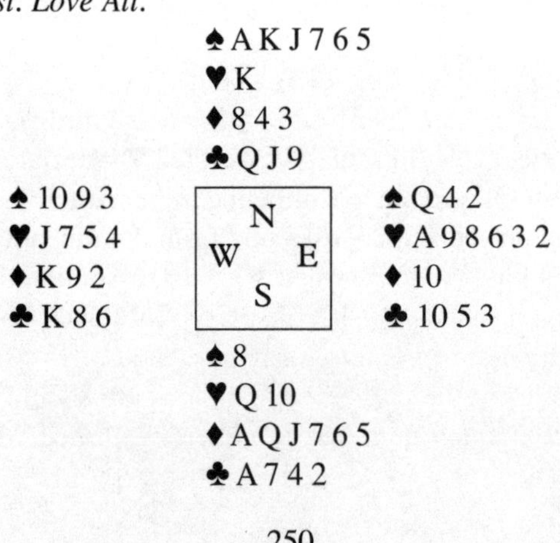

	North	
	♠ A K J 7 6 5 ♥ K ♦ 8 4 3 ♣ Q J 9	
West ♠ 10 9 3 ♥ J 7 5 4 ♦ K 9 2 ♣ K 8 6	N / W E / S	**East** ♠ Q 4 2 ♥ A 9 8 6 3 2 ♦ 10 ♣ 10 5 3
	South ♠ 8 ♥ Q 10 ♦ A Q J 7 6 5 ♣ A 7 4 2	

West	**North**	**East**	**South**
		Pass	1 ♦ (i)
Pass	1 ♥ (ii)	Pass	1 NT (iii)
Pass	2 ♣ (iv)	Pass	2 ♦ (v)
Pass	2 ♥ (vi)	Pass	3 ♦
Pass	3 ♠ (vii)	Pass	3 NT
All Pass			

(i) Normally diamonds, occasionally strong and balanced
(ii) Four of more spades
(iii) Four or more clubs, five or more diamonds
(iv) Relay bid
(vi) Eleven–fifteen high-card points
(vii) Fourth suit

The later dispute centred on the explanations that had occurred sometime around South's bid of Three Diamonds. North thought he had told East 'Five or more diamonds', but East thought the explanation was 'five diamonds'. Meanwhile, South helpfully explained to West that he actually had six diamonds.

The problem was that East did not know what information had been communicated to West, and vice versa, because screens divide the table into two halves. West knew that South's hand had a one–two–six–four shape, and assumed that East knew that too. Unfortunately, East assumed that South was one–three–five–four and needed West to communicate the real layout through defensive play (whereas West assumed East knew the real layout and would put the contract down whatever West did).

The contract of Three No-trumps made at the bridge table but not at the committee table. In actuality, West led ♥4, declarer played the king and East played an encouraging nine rather than the ace. Declarer then played a small diamond from dummy and the finesse lost to West's king. West returned ♥J. East, assuming that declarer had five diamonds and three hearts, played low again. Declarer won with the queen and went on to make nine tricks.

The tournament director ruled that the score should stand. Plus 400 to North–South. That ruling was later overturned. Minus 100 to North–South.

The appeals committee ruling provoked much discussion and opinion was divided on whether they had got the outcome right. Some people argued that East–West did not do well in defence, even allowing for the misinformation. Others pointed out that it would not have been a problem without screens, as all players would have had access to the same information.

The appeal factor has entered many other tournaments. In the 1984 European Junior Championships, France needed to beat Austria 18–12 to win. They won 19–11 but the Austrians appealed against the result on one particular hand where the French had made a slam which could have been defeated. The French had a misunderstanding in the bidding sequence and were unable to explain things clearly. The appeals committee ruled that the result on the board should stand but the French were fined one IMP for an incorrect convention card. This meant the scores of France and Italy were tied, but the French won the Championships because they had beaten the Italians in their match.

A GRAND SLAM FROM FIVE POINTS

SOMEWHERE, SOMEDAY

In many people's opinion, the strangest hand of all is one like this below, where North–South can make Seven Spades from five high-card points. All sorts of close approximations would work just as well. Please let me know if one ever comes up at your table.

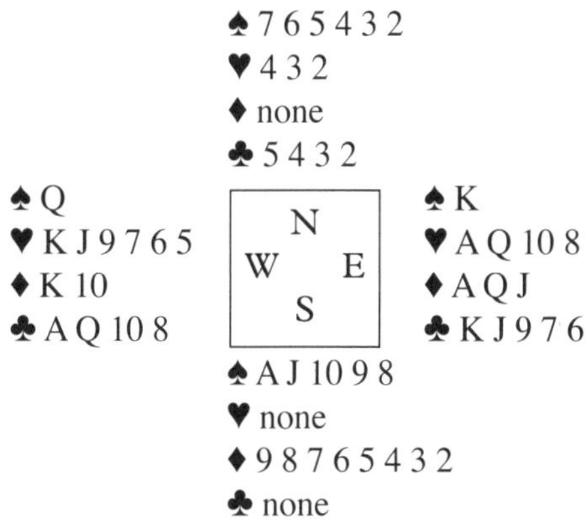

In practice, North–South would have trouble getting a free ride through the bidding, so is it worth having a convention in one's armoury for this purpose? Imagine describing your convention card to opponents: 'We play Weak No-trump, Stayman, Blackwood, Unusual No-trump, Hindsight and the Strange Seven Spade Question.'

JOKER BRIDGE (1)

OXFORD, OCTOBER 2001

When I told one experienced bridge player that I was playing Joker Bridge, he said, 'I think my partner's playing that system too.'

The Joker Bridge variation of the game was devised in the 1930s. It is played with 53 cards – the usual pack plus the joker. The player on dealer's left receives fourteen cards. While they are still face down the dealer slides out one card and keeps it face down on the table. There is a 100-point penalty for exposing the identity of the spare card.

The joker, which can be played at any time, wins any trick. It beats the ace of trumps. A player holding the joker is allowed to discard on one round of trumps and then use the joker to win a later round of trumps. What I'm not sure about is when the joker can be led and whether the player has to name a suit when leading the joker.

The scoring is the same as for bridge, except that the slam bonus was reduced to 200 (small) and 400 (grand) regardless of vulnerability. Slams became much easier for the player with the joker and much harder without it.

Here is an example:

Dealer South.

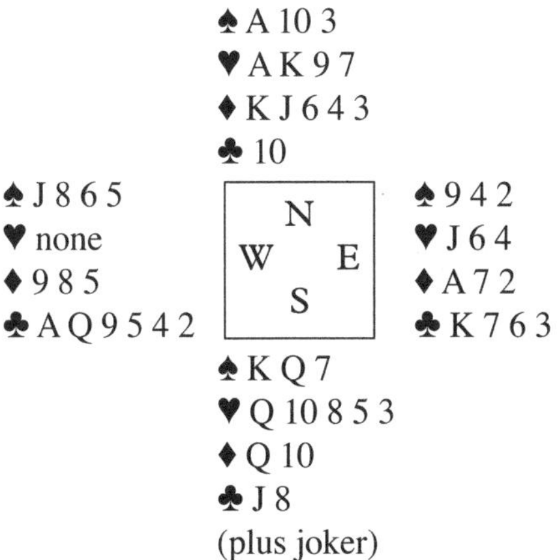

South opened One Heart, and North eventually bid Six Hearts with the help of a hastily contrived Roman Key Card Blackwood Convention which catered for the joker. The two natural losers – one club and one diamond – become one with the aid of the joker. This is an untroubled slam with 25 high-card points, but note that declarer does not know that the missing card is a heart.

After a few hands of Joker Bridge we were all completely flummoxed. What bidding system could show your partner that you have the joker? How many high-card points do you allocate to the joker? How do you cater for the unknown card that has been set aside? When is a losing trick a losing trick?

Certain hands ensure a very odd experience (see page 256).

JOKER BRIDGE (2)

OXFORD, OCTOBER 2001

Here is another strange hand of Joker Bridge. (They all are, I hear you say.) Having the joker goes to South's head and the result is an optimistic contract (Four Hearts). Does any expert joker-bridge player know the best percentage way to play this contract after West's ♣9 lead? If you really want to think about it, you may like to cover up the East–West hands.

Dealer South.

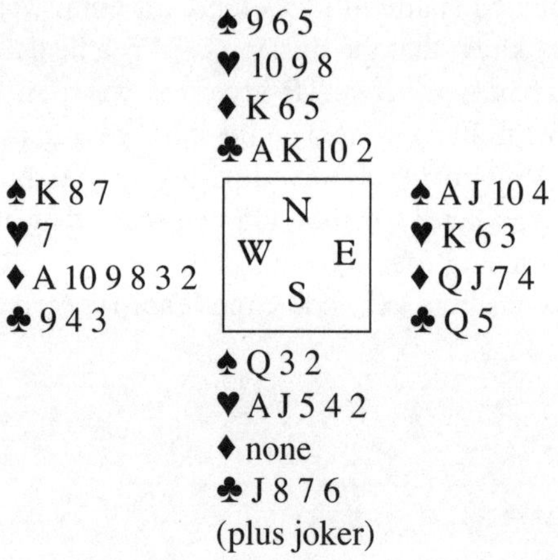

West	**North**	**East**	**South**
			1 ♥
Pass	2 NT	Pass	4 ♥
All Pass			

In practice, South won the first trick with ♣A, then led ♥8 from dummy and let it run. This won the trick and was followed by the nine of trumps, similarly run and won, West discarding ♦8 to ask for a spade. South suspected that either ♥K or ♥Q was the missing card or East would have covered. Or did East have ♥Q and ♥K?

Declarer played ♣K from dummy and the queen fell. The next club was ruffed by East's ♥K for defence's first trick. When East led ♠J, declarer jokered the trick. Declarer conceded the next two tricks to spades but was now sitting pretty with three diamond ruffs, a spade ruff on the table and a winning club.

The lottery of Joker Bridge seems, well, a bit of a joke.

BRIDGE FOR SIX

ENGLAND, 2002

Andrew Potter of Bristol has invented a *Bridge for Six* game which he described in a letter to *Bridge* (Spring 2002).

Three pairs of players sit opposite each other at a table (which is preferably round). The twos are removed from the pack and each player is dealt eight cards.

As Potter explains:

> Bidding proceeds normally, and ceases after five consecutive passes. But whereas normally if the contract is, say, One No-trump, you have to make seven tricks (one over the first six tricks), in *Bridge for Six*, it is only the first trick that does not count. Therefore, a One No-trump contract requires declarer to make two tricks, while for a grand slam all eight tricks are required.

Scoring is the same as for normal bridge (except an extra column is needed). All defenders receive the same penalty points irrespective of who doubles. The lead comes from the player to declarer's left, as in normal bridge, but the next player plays to the trick before dummy goes down.

Here is a specimen hand. Potter sensibly suggests calling the three pairs A, B and C, so I shall adopt that format, even though I quite like the idea of South–West partnering North–East and South–East partnering North–West.

Dealer C2. Love All.

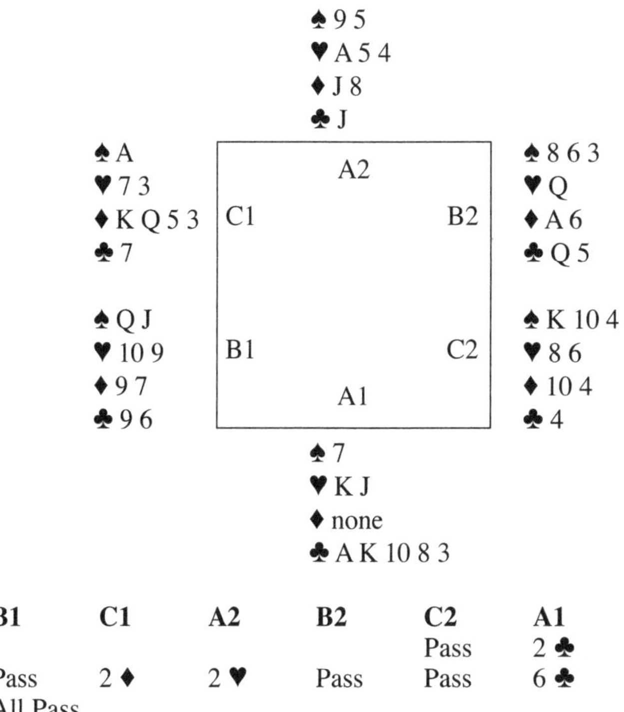

B1	**C1**	**A2**	**B2**	**C2**	**A1**
				Pass	2 ♣
Pass	2 ♦	2 ♥	Pass	Pass	6 ♣
All Pass					

Six-person bidding may strip away the history of conventions, but Andrew Potter points out that fourteen high-card points may give a partnership the majority of points. Bidding can be more competitive in the six-player game, as all players with more than eight points are looking for action.

Here the final contract was Six Clubs (seeking seven tricks) and B1 led ♥10. There is, of course, quite a high likelihood of a void, so declarer was very happy when everyone followed suit to the lead, taking the trick with the king, and even happier to see trumps split two–one–two–one.

After two rounds of trumps, declarer played ♥J, overtaking with the ace. A favourable split in hearts – two–two–one–two – created a winner in dummy and a place for the losing spade. Six Clubs was one over (from seventeen points).

MASSACRE AT THE TABLE

OSLO, NORWAY, FEBRUARY 2002

The game's capacity for strangeness reached a new level in Oslo when all four members of a Saturday-night bridge party were shot dead at the table. No other person was involved.

The four men were all over sixty. The host, Willy Seljelid, was celebrating his 75th birthday when he died at the scene of his bridge game and a 63-year-old friend was also killed immediately. The other two died in hospital later. One, Per Steinar Seljelid, aged 67, was a brother of the host and the other was a 69-year-old.

Police were unable to question any of the men before they died, so the event was shrouded in mystery. A legally registered .22-calibre hunting rifle was found at the scene of the crime but no motive could be established. The police closed the case, presumably because they were convinced that one man had killed the other three before turning the gun on himself.

'Shocked neighbours said they heard quarrelling,' reported the Norwegian newspaper *Aftenposten*. 'But the assailant at the bridge party apparently used a silencer on the gun that ended the argument.'

We will probably never know whether the row was about the game itself. Certainly bridge terminology is full of references to killer leads, sacrifices, endplays and the final contract, but this was surely taking things a bit too far.

However, the Oslo massacre does confirm that bridge will continue to provide us with a fund of bizarre stories, making sure that any collection of strange hands remains incomplete.

HOW TO DEAL A PERFECT HAND

ANY NEW PACK OF CARDS, ANYWHERE IN THE WORLD

Here's one you can try at home.

Take a new pack of cards and remove the jokers. Split the pack into two equal 26-card stacks. Shuffle by flicking down exactly one card from one pack and then exactly one card from the other pack. Take this new pile and split into two more 26-card stacks. Shuffle again by alternating the cards. (Were you to deal now you would create four one-suited hands.) Go through the procedure twice more to show everyone how thoroughly you are shuffling. Then pass the cards over and wait until they are cut.

If you have alternated the cards perfectly in your shuffle, this is how they will be dealt:

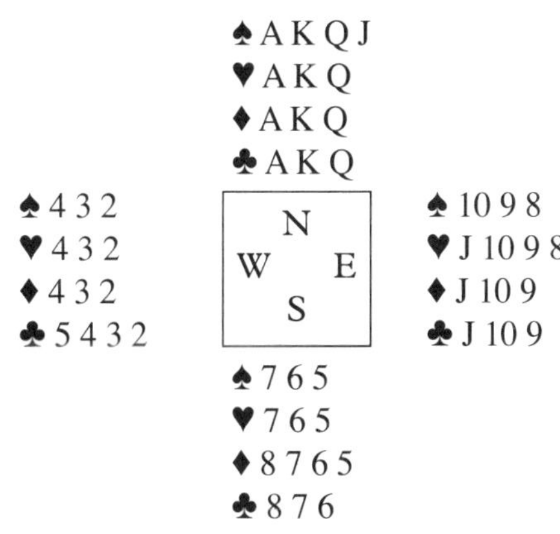

I learned this little trick from an article called 'How Random is Your Bridge Hand?' by Harry Freeman and Len Salmon (*Bridge Magazine*, October 1996).

A word of warning, however. This is something that should only be done as a magic trick at home. If you ever do it in public you may find that your bridge-club committee will give you a lot more time to practise dealing on your own at home.

Selected Bibliography

Anderson, Molly, *Bridge Party Hostess*, 1995
Barton, F P, *We'll Go No More A-Roving*, 1937
Beasley, H M, *Beasley v Culbertson*, 1933
Bird, David, *Famous Bridge Disasters*, 1999
Buller, Walter, *Reflections of a Bridge Player*, 1929
Churchill, R S, *Winston S. Churchill, Vol. 2: Young Statesman, 1901–14*, 1967
Clay, John, *Culbertson: The Man Who Made Contract Bridge*, 1985
Clay, John, *Tales from the Bridge Table*, 1998
Coffin, G S, *Bridge for Three*, 1955
Cohen, Ben and Barrow, Rhoda, *The Bridge Players' Encyclopedia*, 1967
Cole, E R, and Edwards, James, *Grand Slam*, 1975
Cox, Nicola, *The Bridge Players' Supper Book*, 1995
Daniels, David, *Golden Age of Contract Bridge*, 1980
Elwell, Joseph B, *The Analysis and Complete Play of the Bridge Tournament Hands*, 1904
Elwell, Joseph B, *The Play of the Bridge Hands in the One Thousand Dollar Prize Contest*, 1907
Elwell, Joseph B, *Auction Bridge to Date*, 1913
Ewen, R B, *Opening Leads*, 1970
Fleming, Ian, *Moonraker*, 1955
Forrester, Tony, *Vintage Forrester: Selected Writings from the Daily Telegraph*, 1998
Foster, R F, *Foster's Contract Bridge*, 1927

Fox, G C H, *Sound Bidding at Contract*, 1954

Fox, G C H, *Grand Master of Bridge – Foxy: The Autobiography of G C H Fox*, 1999

Fox Sheinwold, Patricia, *Husbands and Other Men I've Played With*, 1979

Francis, Henry and Senior, Brian, *The Bermuda Bowl: History and the All Time Best Deals*, 1999

Francis, Henry and Truscott, Alan, *The Official Encyclopedia of Bridge*, 1994

Fry, Samuel, and Hymes, Edward, *How to Win at Five Suit Bridge*, 1938

Griffiths, J N R, *The Golden Years of Bridge*, 1981

Harrison-Gray, Maurice, *The Country Life Book of Bridge*, 1972

Hart, Norman de V, *The Bridge Player's Bedside Book*, 1939

Hervey, G F, *The Bridge Player's Bedside Book*, 1964

Horton, Mark, *The Mammoth Book of Bridge*, 1999

Hughes, Spike, *The Art of Coarse Bridge*, 1970

Le Dentu, José, *Bridge: Triumphs and Disasters*, 1990

Loring-Bruce, Arthur, *The Bridge Fiend*, 1909

Mackay, Rex, *The Walk of the Oysters: The Unholy History of Contract Bridge*, 1986

Mahmood, Zia, *Bridge My Way*, 1991

Markus, Rixi, *Bridge Around the World*, 1978

Markus, Rixi, *More Deadlier Than the Male*, 1984

Markus, Rixi, *A Vulnerable Game: The Memoirs of Rixi Marcus*, 1988

Mollo, Victor, *Confessions of an Addict*, 1966

Mollo, Victor, *The Bridge Immortals*, 1967

Mollo, Victor, *The Other Side of Bridge*, 1984

Nicolet, C C, *Death of a Bridge Expert*, 1933

Phillips, Hubert, *You Can Play and Laugh*, 1934

Phillips, Hubert, *Complete Contract Bridge*, 1948

Phillips, Hubert, *Bridge is Only a Game*, 1961

Poullada, Leon, *Reform and Rebellion in Afghanistan, 1919–29*, 1973

Proctor, Richard A, *How to Play Whist*, 1885

Reese, Terence, *Story of an Accusation*, 1966

Reese, Terence, *Bridge at the Top*, 1977
Reese, Terence and Bird, David, *Famous Hands from Famous Matches*, 1991
Rosenberg, Mike, *Bridge, Zia and Me*, 1999
Sheehan, Robert, *The Times Book of Bridge 1*, 1997
Sheehan, Robert, *The Times Book of Bridge 2*, 1998
Simon, S, *Design for Bidding*, 1949
Sims, Dorothy, *Psychic Bidding*, 1932
Smith, Marc, *Man vs. Machine*, 1999
Smith, Nick, *Bridge Literature*, 1993
Sontag, Alan, *The Bridge Bum*, 1977
Stern, Paul, *Beating the Culbertsons: How the Austrians Won the World Contract Bridge Championship*, 1938
Truscott, Alan, *The Great Bridge Scandal*, 1967